THE LAW
IN 60
SECONDS

THE LAW IN 60 SECONDS

A POCKET GUIDE TO YOUR RIGHTS

CHRISTIAN WEAVER

PROFILE BOOKS

First published in Great Britain in 2021 by
Profile Books Ltd
29 Cloth Fair
London
ECIA 7JQ
www.profilebooks.com

3 5 7 9 10 8 6 4 2

Typeset in Dante by MacGuru Ltd
Printed and bound in Great Britain by
CPI Group (UK) Ltd, Croydon, CR0 4YY

A CIP catalogue record for this book is available from the British Library.

ISBN 978 1 78816 649 2
eISBN 978 1 78283 767 1

Contents

Introduction

What would you do if your landlord changed the locks and you could no longer access your home? Would you know the law?

Would you know how you legally are able to respond if bailiffs came knocking on your door?

If your younger brother called from a police station, could you tell him his rights?

For many of us the answer to these questions would be 'no', forcing us to rely on the goodwill of those exerting their power over us, whether that be the landlord, bailiff or police officer. Not knowing the law might not always be the end of the world – perhaps it just means you lose £10 because you don't challenge the guy at customer services who says you're not entitled to a refund. But those small instances add up, building a world where we're not really in control, where we're not sure of our rights or our protections. When it comes to more important interactions such as those involving our jobs, housing or freedom – the consequences can be huge.

Wherever your legal issue lies on the scale of seriousness – this book is here to help.

The Law in 60 Seconds: A Pocket Guide to Your Rights is a practical and intuitive guide to your legal rights and entitlements, covering everything from housing and money, to healthcare, travel and shopping, to drugs and alcohol, and protesting. It serves as the 'lawyer friend' it would be handy to have on WhatsApp. Treat this book as your trusty companion, contactable at any hour of the day to provide guidance on everyday legal queries.

This book is for anyone and everyone – after all, whenever you leave the house (and even if you don't), you're engaging with invisible laws, some that will work in your favour, and others that might not. Sometimes the law protects us, and this book will help you find out how to use it to resolve conflicts, claim your rights and keep yourself safe. Sometimes the law prevents us from doing things, and this book will also help you work out where the boundaries are – and what to do if you end up crossing them.

The genesis of the idea for this book came from a feeling of powerlessness. I was in my early twenties, had not long finished Law School and was soon to start my training to become a barrister (known as pupillage). I was living in London and knife crime was once again dominating the news agenda with stop and search being suggested as the best solution. I felt extremely uneasy at the growing calls for its increased use.

As a Black person, I am around nine times more likely to be stopped and searched by police than a white person. Therefore, I knew any increase in the use of this policing tool (which, particularly when done improperly, can be deeply humiliating and at times traumatising for the recipient) was likely to have a disproportionate effect on me and many of my peers.

Drawing on knowledge I had picked up over the course of my legal education, I decided to record a short video on the topic of stop and search for my friends (and, actually, as a form of revision for myself). While I couldn't stop my friends being stopped and searched, I could make sure they knew their rights if they were. I called the video 'The Law in 60 Seconds' and placed it on YouTube.

The response was overwhelming. People found it useful. They sent it to their friends, siblings and children; they bookmarked the link on their web browsers. Soon the video had amassed its first thousand views. It was featured in mainstream media multiple times. I made videos on other important-to-know legal rights, such as those you have as a tenant, as a consumer, and when at a protest.

It was never the plan to turn The Law in 60 Seconds into a book, but the impact that these grainy homemade videos were having on viewers was clear, and, as the number of topics I wanted to cover grew, a book that could offer more in-depth analysis seemed the logical next step. I started The Law in 60 Seconds as a 'student' of the law – regularly reading legal updates in preparation for the commencement of my pupillage. I am now a fully-fledged barrister working daily *within* the law.

As a lawyer typically representing the person/organisation that doesn't hold the balance of power (the tenant as opposed to the landlord, the asylum seeker as opposed to the Home Office, the accused as opposed to the Crown Prosecution Service, etc.), I often find myself wishing I could give my clients something a little more permanent after their appearance in court to help them find their footing in this world. This book contains all of the information I would want to give to a client when saying those fleeting words, 'best of luck moving forward'.

How to use this book

Phone – check. Keys – check. *The Law in 60 Seconds* – check.

Call it ambitious – but I see no place more appropriate for this book than on your person wherever you go. Maybe you'll have two copies – one for home and one for your bag – a bit like your phone charger. Maybe you'll keep a copy in the glove compartment of your car. This lightweight book enables you to have essential legal information at your fingertips, available at all times.

Pulled over by the police in a traffic stop? You know your rights.

In a taxi and suspect you're being overcharged? This book will give you important pointers.

I would hope for it to be so full of your own personal notes, highlighting, tabs, scuffs and scrapes that you not only are able to speedily access the sections particularly relevant to your own life, but would genuinely be upset if you lost it too.

The book is split into chapters, each covering a different broad topic. Within each one, you'll find information on situations that might occur, important principles to know beforehand and what you can do to tackle any problems that might arise. You will also find sections marked with tick symbols appearing throughout the book. These ticks will provide you with quick nuggets of information; pointing out key hacks, tips, tricks or otherwise useful things I think you ought to know.

I have focused on information that will be most practical for people under 40, who typically may rent (rather than own) their house or flat and who are employed rather than an employer. Nonetheless, much of what is here will be relevant no matter your age or stage in life. In fact, if you're an employer, this book may help you be the great, fair boss that gets the best out of her employees.

I'm not an expert in every area of law and although other experts have reviewed and approved the content, **this book is not legal advice** and in no way seeks to substitute speaking to a lawyer about your personal circumstance. However, it is hoped that, as a first port of call, this book will give you confidence in situations where the power balance feels skewed. If this book helps you walk with your back that bit straighter, and with a little more swagger in your step, assured in the knowledge that you have the ability to deal with typical day-to-day legal issues that might arise – my mission has been accomplished.

The law detailed in this book is 'English law' – in other words, the law covering England and Wales. Notwithstanding this, there may be small regional differences, and some of the practical tips suggested will have greater applicability in one region compared to the other. Therefore, it is always important to double-check how things operate where you live.

Knowledge is power, and I hope you finish this book feeling empowered.

Preface

Your Human Rights

As a barrister working in the field of human rights, my goal is to make the law work for ordinary people, not just those who have the money or 'know how' to utilise it to its full effect. Part of this comes from knowing what it is like to feel as if the law is not on your side. One of my earliest childhood memories is of dog faeces being smeared over my grandparents' car on their driveway in weekly, sustained, racist attacks. I was 6 at the time. Despite calls from my parents to the police detailing the devastating effect this racist abuse was having on my grandparents, the racists were not found and my grandparents were left feeling violated in the parameters of their own home. As a family we rallied together, and, led by my grandfather, were able to get press coverage of what was going on. Soon enough, the racist incidents stopped. Nonetheless, from a young age, I remember having an appreciation way beyond my years of what it felt like to be powerless. With this in mind, I seek to empower you with each and every page of this book, beginning with your human rights.

Human rights are rights that we are all born with, no matter where we're from, what we look like, what we believe, or how we live. They are freedoms and protections that can never be taken away from us. And they're not just nice ideals: they're also defined and protected by law.

So, if there is one section that is important to read in this book – it is this one. It will not only arm you with the knowledge of your inalienable rights, but also provide you with a helpful legal foundation and explain principles and concepts that are relevant in later chapters.

The Human Rights Act 1998

Following the Second World War, there was a desire to prevent the horrors of that war from ever being repeated. The result was the Universal Declaration of Human Rights. This was a document, set out by the United Nations and agreed by an international community, that defined the fundamental rights and freedoms that every human being in the world should have at a minimum. It was signed into effect in 1948 and is still in place today.

It is from this foundation that the European Convention on Human Rights (ECHR) was created in 1950. This document protects the human rights of people in countries that belong to the Council of Europe – of which the UK is one. (It's important to note that the Council of Europe is an international human rights organisation, and is *not* the same as the European Union – which, of course, the UK is no longer part of.)

In the UK, our rights are protected by the Human Rights Act 1998. The Act makes most of the rights in the ECHR part of our own UK law. It is important that the UK has its own Act that protects human rights, because it means that any breaches can be dealt with in a UK court. If we didn't have this and we could rely only on the rights as protected by the ECHR, we'd have to go to the European Court of Human Rights – which is all the way in Strasbourg, France.

Who must follow the Human Rights Act?

The Human Rights Act *must* be followed by public authorities. Public authorities are bodies that provide services or carry out functions that are in the public interest: e.g. the NHS, government departments, local authorities, police departments and the courts, to name a few. They are obliged to ensure that they act in a way that is compatible with your human rights at all times – whether this is when making specific decisions about you, or when making policy or service decisions that may affect many people. Although not strictly speaking public authorities, any private organisation carrying out public functions – such as Network Rail or a utility company – must also act in a manner compatible with your human rights.

What are your human rights?

The history part of this chapter over, we can turn to the most important question: what actually are your rights under the Human Rights Act? Well, the Human Rights Act contains sixteen rights/freedoms/protections that derive from the ECHR.* These are as follows:

Article 2: Right to life

Article 3: Freedom from torture and inhuman or degrading treatment or punishment

Article 4: Freedom from slavery and forced labour

Article 5: Right to liberty and security

Article 6: Right to a fair trial

Article 7: No punishment without law

Article 8: Respect for your private and family life, home and correspondence

Article 9: Freedom of thought, conscience and religion

Article 10: Freedom of expression

Article 11: Freedom of peaceful assembly and association

Article 12: Right to marry and start a family

---

* Articles 1 and 13 of the ECHR, ensuring that states must secure the rights of the Convention in their own jurisdiction (1), and that if someone's rights are violated they are able to access effective remedy, i.e. take their case to court (13), do not feature in the Act; by creating the Human Rights Act, the UK has fulfilled these rights.

Article 14: Protection from discrimination in respect of these rights
    and freedoms

Protocol 1, Article 1: Right to peaceful enjoyment of your property

Protocol 1, Article 2: Right to education

Protocol 1, Article 3: Right to participate in free elections

Protocol 13, Article 1: Abolition of the death penalty

A lot of the titles of these articles seem fairly self-explanatory – but of course they hide complexities. To give you more of a sense of what these actually mean in practice, let's have a look at some of them in more detail.

Article 2: Right to life

Article 2 protects your right to life. Public authorities cannot take your life and exceptions are allowed only if the force used was 'absolutely necessary' (such as to protect somebody else's life). Protecting the right to life also means that where someone has died in unexplained circumstances, particularly if they were under the responsibility of the state, there will be an effective and official investigation to ascertain how they died. The state also has a 'positive obligation' to protect you against other individuals who it learns wish to do you harm, for example through effective policing.

Article 3: Freedom from torture and inhuman or degrading treatment or punishment

Article 3 is the right to be free from torture and inhuman or degrading treatment or punishment. Public authorities cannot inflict this treatment on you. They also have a positive duty to protect you from others who might be treating you in the same way. Therefore, if, for example, a local authority learns that a child is at risk of abuse or neglect from its parent, failure to intervene could amount to a breach of Article 3. Article 3 has implications for everyone in the UK, including those seeking asylum. If the authorities want to remove or deport somebody to another country, they breach Article 3 if they do so with the belief that the person will be tortured (or will receive inhuman or degrading treatment or punishment) upon arrival in that country. An example might be where a person has fled a country over fears they will be killed due to their sexual orientation, and would still be at risk if returned. It would be against the law for the UK to remove that person.

Article 5: Right to liberty and security

Article 5 protects you from arbitrary and unlawful detention. This means that unless there is good reason you must not be imprisoned or detained. Even in situations where you are legally detained (e.g. if you are rightfully arrested), if the police then detain you for longer than they are legally allowed, this could amount to a breach of Article 5. Potential breaches of Article 5 can also occur when it comes to detention in, among other places, mental health hospitals and care homes. If you are arrested, you should be told the reasons for your arrest.

Article 6: Right to a fair trial

Article 6 is the right to a fair trial. This means a public hearing by an impartial court, within a reasonable time. You have this right whether you are a defendant in criminal proceedings, or a decision is being made that will have an impact on your civil rights or obligations. Article 6 states that, in relation to criminal proceedings, everyone charged with a criminal offence is to be presumed innocent until proven guilty. Among other things, it entitles those charged with a criminal offence to free legal representation if they cannot afford it and it is in the interests of justice.

Article 8: Respect for your private and family life, home and correspondence

Article 8 is the right to respect for your private and family life, home and correspondence. This means you can live your life privately and without state interference, apart from in very limited circumstances as set out in the second paragraph of Article 8. The meaning of private life is broad, and includes things such as your right to lead the lifestyle you want, as well as the right to decide who can see and touch your body and your sexual orientation. Your family life includes your right to have family relationships and to live and maintain contact with family. Along with a number of other groups and individuals, unmarried couples can be included within family life. Your right to your home is not the right to housing, but to peacefully enjoy the home you currently live in.

Your correspondence includes your letters, texts and emails. Article 8 also protects you from unjustified surveillance by state authorities such as the police, and creates rigorous rules for situations where the police wish to process your data for technologies such as biometric scanning and facial recognition cameras.

Article 9: Freedom of thought, conscience and religion

Article 9 protects your right to freedom of thought, conscience and religion. This includes your right to hold beliefs. These beliefs need not be religious and could include veganism or atheism. You have the right to change your religion or beliefs whenever you please. You also have the right to manifest and practise your religion and beliefs without interference from a public authority, apart from in very limited circumstances as set out in the second paragraph of Article 9.

Article 14: Protection from discrimination in respect of these rights and freedoms

Article 14 is protection from discrimination in connection with your other rights in the Convention (as opposed to in all areas of your life). In other words, Article 14 protects you from being discriminated against in enjoying your rights as set out in the Convention. In terms of more general discrimination protection that can apply to other aspects of your life, this is provided for in other legislation, such as the Equality Act 2010.

This selection details the rights most likely to be of use to the typical reader. Other Articles are also important to know, and some of these will be covered in other chapters; for example, Chapter 10, on activism, will touch on freedom of expression (Article 10) – which includes your freedom of speech – as well as freedom of peaceful assembly and association (Article 11). Remember, private individuals and private companies *do not* have to follow the Act – so you can't argue Article 5 because you got stuck in the lift at your local shopping centre. You also couldn't argue Article 8 against Barbara, the annoying neighbour at number 42, who cheekily once read a letter addressed to you but posted through her letter box. Nonetheless, as you will see throughout this book, there are plenty of other laws that exist to help you deal with some of the troubling and on occasion downright odd things that people do in this world. These laws are often long established within English law, having developed slowly and incrementally over hundreds of years.

It's worth emphasising one more time that *all of us* have human rights and we should have them respected. You could be in prison, homeless, an asylum seeker or an 'Average Joe'. No matter the colour of your skin, your language, your size or age, your abilities, your nationality, your sexuality or gender identity, your political or religious beliefs, you benefit from the Human Rights Act 1998.

Types of rights

Even though we do all have these rights, it is important to be aware that there are situations where a public authority *can* interfere with your human rights.

In order to understand why that's the case, you need to know that there are three categories of rights: absolute, limited and qualified.

Absolute rights can never be infringed – no ifs, no buts. Article 3 (your right to freedom from torture and inhuman or degrading treatment or punishment) is an example of an absolute right. No matter the circumstance, or whatever the seeming justification may be, you absolutely have this protection.

Limited rights are rights that can be restricted in certain specific situations. Article 5 (your right to liberty and security) is a good example. We understand that despite having this right, prisons still exist. Along with the right, there follows a set of specific limitations to it. Any limitation that is not explicitly stated in the Article cannot be used to infringe upon this right. An excerpt from Article 5 is as follows:

> 1. *Everyone has the right to liberty and security of person. No one shall be deprived of his liberty **save in the following cases and in accordance with a procedure prescribed by law:***
>
> (a) *the lawful detention of a person after conviction by a competent court;*
> (b) *the lawful arrest or detention of a person for non-compliance*

*with the lawful order of a court or in order to secure the ful-
filment of any obligation prescribed by law;*

*(c) the lawful arrest or detention of a person effected for the
purpose of bringing him before the competent legal authority on reasonable suspicion of having committed an offence
or when it is reasonably considered necessary to prevent his
committing an offence or fleeing after having done so;*

*(d) the detention of a minor by lawful order for the purpose
of educational supervision or his lawful detention for
the purpose of bringing him before the competent legal
authority;*

*(e) the lawful detention of persons for the prevention of the
spreading of infectious diseases, of persons of unsound
mind, alcoholics or drug addicts or vagrants;*

*(f) the lawful arrest or detention of a person to prevent his
effecting an unauthorised entry into the country or of a
person against whom action is being taken with a view to
deportation or extradition.*

[…]

This excerpt allows us to clearly see the instances where the
state can lawfully interfere with this right. Unless for a reason
stipulated in the Article, the state cannot infringe upon this
right.

Qualified rights must strike a balance between your rights
as an individual and the rights of other individuals and/or the
general public. Any infringement on a qualified right must
be 'necessary in a democratic society'; for example, in the

interests of national security or public safety. Any infringement must also be proportionate – in other words, infringing on the right only as much as is needed, and no more. Article 8 (your right to respect for your private and family life, home and correspondence) is a good example of a qualified right. An excerpt from it is as follows:

> [...]
>
> 2. *There shall be no interference by a public authority with the exercise of this right except such as is in accordance with the law and is necessary in a democratic society in the interests of national security, public safety or the economic wellbeing of the country, for the prevention of disorder or crime, for the protection of health or morals, or for the protection of the rights and freedoms of others.*

The 'interests' listed above, such as national security and public safety, are known as 'legitimate aims'. Any infringement on the Article must be designed to promote a specific legitimate aim.

Taking action under the Human Rights Act

Public bodies, by virtue of being public bodies, should always be alert to issues relating to human rights and have them in mind when making decisions. They risk breaking the law if they do not.

If you ever feel like your human rights have been infringed, and that you want to do something about it, there are options available to you.

You may consider writing a complaint about the issue to the organisation. A firm complaint letter showing an awareness of your rights may resolve the issue. See Chapter 12 for suggestions on how this can be done as well as other considerations.

If you choose to take legal action, be aware that you usually would need to bring a claim within 1 year of the potential human rights breach. Depending on the type of court action you take, you may have even as little as 3 months. Such an example is a legal process known as 'judicial review' where a court will examine the decision or action of a public body and consider whether they acted lawfully.

By knowing your human rights, you have a strong foundational sense of how all of your interactions with public authorities should go. Become familiar with them, they are yours.

While your rights under the Human Rights Act will rear their head occasionally over the course of the book, the primary focus from this point on is arming you with your rights in the everyday situations that don't involve public authorities.

1

Renting

Considering he fails repeatedly to return my calls, my landlord receives a shockingly large proportion of my income. Maybe yours does too: on average, people in England spend over 45 per cent of their income on rent. And it's not just the rent that's expensive; even for the most seasoned of renters, the figures on the council tax bill have a strange way of always taking you by surprise – despite their predictability.

My landlord and I are still on our journey towards a better relationship, but this chapter is all about helping *you* foster a positive relationship with *your* landlord, or, where this is not possible (as will sometimes be the case), a relationship that ensures you do not get walked all over. It might be the case that all of your previous landlords have been a joy. If so – great – but this chapter will prepare you for the one that is not.

Renting involves money, sometimes it involves relationships, but at its foundation, it is nearly always about shelter. Home is where you should feel safe and secure. Knowing your rights around renting means not only potentially saving money, and saving relationships with your housemates (more on this later), but also making sure that where you go home to sleep doesn't become a nightmare.

In this chapter, we will walk through the basics of the most common type of tenancy for those privately renting – the assured shorthold tenancy – discussing the things you need to know to safeguard both your money and your sanity. We will also look at the things that, while not directly related to your landlord or renting, *are* related to your overall experience of living in a house or flat. After all, nobody likes to be in the dark when it comes to matters as serious as their utility company disconnecting the energy supply.

The basics

Before you can kick off your shoes in the home you hope to occupy as a tenant, you'll need to sign a tenancy agreement (a contract between you and your landlord). This is something worth taking seriously – even if it's your hundredth time signing one. There's always a first time for things to go wrong. If you think reading the tenancy agreement carefully sounds boring, just remember that your landlord knows this stuff. Do you really want all the power to be in their hands?

Throughout this chapter, for ease of reading, when I refer to the 'landlord', I will also be referring to any agents acting on their behalf.

The focus of this chapter is exclusively the most common type of tenancy for those privately renting: the assured short-hold tenancy (AST). If you don't live with your landlord, your tenancy started on or after 28 February 1997, and you aren't paying rent of more than £100,000 a year or less than £250 a year (less than £1,000 in London), you will usually have an AST.

About to sign a tenancy agreement? Here are some things to consider and look out for

CHECK: How long are you 'tied in' to the contract for?

For an AST, the contract will likely contain a fixed period of time (a **'fixed term'**) that the tenancy will last for, e.g. 6 months or 12 months. You will have to pay the rent until at least the end of the fixed term unless an agreement can be reached with your landlord or your contract allows you to end the tenancy early (i.e. through a break clause – more on this later). Once the fixed term is over, a **periodic tenancy** will often automatically come into place. This is where the tenancy rolls over on a weekly or monthly basis. If you wish to leave a periodic tenancy, you will usually need to give at least 1 month's notice if your rent is due monthly, or 4 weeks' notice if it is weekly. Before you sign, double-check your contract to ensure that you will not be required to give more notice than this (look for a heading in the contract stating 'Notice period' or something similar). If you will be required to give more notice than this and you think this could be a problem, now is your chance to say.

CHECK: Is there a 'break clause' in the tenancy agreement?

A break clause is a clause in the tenancy agreement enabling either party – whether that be you (the tenant) or the landlord – to give notice (i.e. advance warning) to terminate the tenancy agreement before the end of the fixed term. The amount of notice that needs to be given should be clearly stated in the break clause. If a break clause is not included and you think this flexibility is important, consider asking for one to be put in. Just remember that your landlord can also make use of the break clause if they want to get rid of you.

CONSIDER: Will you be a 'sole tenant' or a 'joint tenant'?

You are a sole tenant if the tenancy agreement you are currently looking at is in your name only. Simple. Don't let the fact that you may be moving into a property where others currently live confuse you. You can be a sole tenant and still live with others. A prime example of this is where each person has exclusive possession of a specific room – perhaps 'bedroom 2' is your room only, but you and others will share the kitchen and bathroom. If you are to be a sole tenant, have a look at the section entitled 'Life as a sole tenant' (p. 29) so you have an idea of what your rights and responsibilities will be.

You are a joint tenant if, along with others, you all sign your names on one single tenancy agreement. This is a typical scenario for friends at university renting a house together. In this situation, rather than signing a contract for a room (as shown in the example above), you all sign a contract for the house, and then argue over who gets the best bedroom. If you are to be a joint tenant, have a look at the section entitled 'Life as a joint tenant' (p. 26) so you have an idea of what your rights and responsibilities will be.

Moving in day? Here's a checklist of things to make sure you receive from the landlord

- The most recent copy of the government guide *How to rent: the checklist for renting in England*. This provides helpful information for you as a tenant and gets you on a steady footing as to what to expect from your landlord and what they can expect from you. (Note that there is no equivalent of this in Wales.)
- If your property has a gas installation or appliance, you must be given a gas safety certificate before you physically move in. You must then be given a copy of the new certificate after each annual gas safety check.
- A copy of the Energy Performance Certificate (EPC), which tells you the energy performance rating of your property. This might not sound very exciting, but it often contains handy recommendations on how you can save energy – and thus save money.
- A record of any electrical inspections and an electrical safety report (usually an Electrical Installation Condition Report). (There is no requirement to provide an electrical

safety report in Wales, but landlords are still required to provide a property that meets electrical standards, including safe installations and appliances.)
- Evidence that the smoke alarms and any carbon monoxide alarms work. (England only.)
- If you have paid the landlord a deposit, they must 'protect' it by placing it in a government-approved tenancy deposit protection scheme. The landlord will then have to provide you with 'prescribed information' in relation to your deposit (see p. 41 for more information). This must be issued within 30 days of the landlord receiving it (so will not necessarily be on your moving in day).

Bills: some guidance

Whether you are in a sole or joint tenancy, it is likely you will be responsible for paying bills.

If all of your names appear on a utility bill: the supplier can pursue any of you for money.

If only your name appears on a utility bill: you are legally responsible for the whole bill. If your housemates do not pay you their share, you will still need to pay the full amount. With this in mind, it's a good idea to request that your housemates set up a standing order so there is always money in your account ready for the payment of the bills.

Life as a joint tenant

Entering a joint tenancy is a brilliant character-building exercise. Because of their very nature, joint tenancies tend to be made between friends – or at least a group of people all signing up to live together – and so the pressure is on to keep those relationships working; if not, it could be more than just the tenancy ending. As a result, life as a joint tenant is a bit like a game of chess: you have to think tactically. Leaving Fred outside in the cold may seem like a good way to remind him to take his keys with him on a night out, but because it is from your bank account that the landlord receives the rent, you need to maintain good relations so Fred doesn't cancel his standing order payment to your account. (Note: this section is not applicable to sole tenants who live with others, who will have signed a different type of contract.)

'Lead tenant'

With several people in a property, it makes sense for one of the joint tenants to be the representative for everybody else. This person is known as the 'lead tenant' – an informal term as opposed to a legal one. The lead tenant will be the point of contact for the deposit protection scheme (more on this later) and is usually (but does not have to be) the individual who collects the others' shares of the joint rent before paying the full amount to the landlord. They may also take responsibility for paying household bills such as council tax and utility bills – collecting contributions from the others.

Rent and deposit

As joint tenants, you are all equally responsible for paying the rent. Although the landlord will usually expect payment from the lead tenant, they can legally pursue any of you for the full rent. In other words, if Aleesha loses her job and there is a shortfall in the rent amount, the landlord can pursue any of you for the remainder of it. It does not specifically need to be Aleesha.

You are also all jointly responsible for not damaging the property. If Hassan damages the wall in his bedroom when trying to rearrange the furniture, the costs of fixing it will be deducted by the landlord from the single deposit amount you jointly paid in.

Leaving the property during the fixed term

If every individual in the joint tenancy wants to end the fixed term tenancy early, you can together use the break clause in your contract (if there is one) to give notice, or you could negotiate with the landlord. If this is not possible, although you can physically all walk out of the property, the landlord can still pursue you all for the outstanding rent as the tenancy will not legally have ended.

If you personally need to move out during the fixed term, but the other joint tenants want to stay, the landlord can still pursue you for rent as the tenancy will not legally have ended. You may wish to consider finding somebody willing to replace you as a tenant (ensuring that all of the tenants staying on and your landlord agree to this). If a replacement tenant moves in, it is worth doing your best to ensure that that person signs a *new* tenancy agreement with everybody else who stayed on. This will mean that the tenancy agreement you were a part of no longer exists, and with you not being a part of the new tenancy agreement, your landlord cannot pursue you for rent in relation to it.

Leaving the property outside of the fixed term

If on the last day of your fixed term contract you *all* leave the property, your tenancy will usually end automatically. Double-check your agreement, though, as it may state you have to give notice.

If you choose to leave but others choose to stay, the tenancy will automatically continue as a periodic tenancy. Because the tenancy will not legally have ended, you can still be pursued by the landlord to pay rent. It is therefore important to know that, once in the periodic part of the tenancy, you can give notice to end the tenancy without the permission of your fellow joint tenants. This will end the tenancy for everybody. Notice must be at least 1 month (for monthly periodic tenancies) or 28 days (for weekly tenancies) and must end on the last or first day of a period of the tenancy. If the rest of the joint tenants wish to remain in the property, they should contact the landlord to start a new tenancy agreement without your name on it.

✓If you are in a joint tenancy, your landlord cannot specifically ask *you* to leave. The only way the landlord could get you out is by ending the tenancy for everyone using the eviction process.

Life as a sole tenant

What about sole tenants? It might be just you living in a property, or perhaps you are sharing with others but all of you have your own individual tenancy agreement with the landlord – in other words, you are in possession of 'bedroom 2' but share the kitchen and bathroom with others. Here are some helpful pointers.

Payment of rent

You, and only you, are liable to pay the rent. Failure to pay may lead the landlord to take action against you.

If you are in a shared property, your failure to pay the rent will not in any way impact those you are sharing with.

Leaving the property during the fixed term

You will have to pay rent until at least the end of your fixed term unless you have a break clause in the tenancy agreement, or your landlord agrees to end your tenancy early. While you could physically walk away from the property, the landlord can still pursue you for rent until your tenancy has ended.

If you are in a shared property, your leaving of the property will not have an impact on anybody else.

Your rights to privacy and communal space if sharing with others

If 'bedroom 2' of a property is yours, you have exclusive possession of this room. In other words, it is yours and yours only. You will then share the other facilities, such as the kitchen and bathroom. Therefore, while you will have control over what goes on in 'bedroom 2', compromise will be needed to ensure that you all coexist peacefully in the shared areas of the property.

Living conditions

As a tenant, you have rights. You have the right to live in accommodation without rats running under the sofa, or where you are suffocated by the smell of damp. You have the right to feel safe, and for the property to be secure. Although the landlord owns the property, they can't just barge in whenever they like. You are the tenant and it is not just a question of courtesy, but it is your *right* to have advance warning. The problem is that all too many tenants live in conditions that are frankly illegal because they do not know their rights and certain landlords think they can get away with it. Don't let your landlord be one of them.

Homes must be 'fit for human habitation'

You have the right to live in a home that is 'fit for human habitation'.

A home will be deemed 'unfit for human habitation' if conditions are so bad that the home is unsuitable for you to live in while in that condition. Examples include fire safety issues, security issues (e.g. not having a lock on your front door), hygiene or sanitation issues (e.g. not having a working toilet), and infestations (e.g. cockroaches or mice).

✓ This, strictly speaking, applies in relation to England only. While homes being fit for human habitation features in the Renting Homes (Wales) Act 2016, at the time of writing, this is not in force. As applies to much of this book – the organisations listed in the back pages will be well placed to advise on avenues for you to consider based on your situation.

Homes must be 'kept in repair'

It is your landlord's responsibility to carry out basic repairs. If the problem in your home is not quite one that makes it unfit to live in, then your best option may involve looking into the 'Repairing obligations' provisions from the Landlord and Tenant Act 1985.

Regardless of what is in your tenancy agreement, your landlord has a general responsibility to 'keep in repair' the following:

- the structure and exterior of your house; for example, the drains, gutters and external pipes
- basins, sinks, baths and toilets
- boilers, heaters and their associated pipes and wiring

If your landlord stated additional things in your tenancy agreement that they would do in terms of repair obligations, they must stick to these. Another reason to read the tenancy agreement carefully.

If you feel your landlord is ignoring these responsibilities

If you believe your home is not fit for human habitation, or that repairs need to be made, you should tell your landlord as soon as possible. It is best to do this in writing (letter, email or text) and keep a copy as evidence. If you are particularly concerned, you may also wish to tell the local council, as it has legal powers it can use to get repairs done very quickly.

Once your landlord is aware of the problem, they have a duty to repair it within a reasonable amount of time. Exactly what the problem is and its severity will have a bearing on what will be classed as a reasonable amount of time.

If this does not happen, it can be a good idea to write to your landlord again, stating:

- what the problem is
- the history of your communication (i.e. when you reported it and what you were told – highlighting that this hasn't happened)
- the impact this is having, being sure to detail any inconvenience and potential implications for your health

If all else fails, you may wish to consider legal action. A

court can order that your landlord pay you compensation and/or carry out the necessary repairs. Court should be a last resort: it can be much quicker to negotiate and come to an agreement with your landlord. Before going to court, it is a good idea to speak to your local Citizens Advice (see p. 278) or a housing lawyer for advice.

✓The need to inform your landlord as soon as possible if you think repairs are needed cannot be stressed enough. If you do not, and what would have been a minor repair becomes a much larger one, your deposit may be at risk. Many tenancy agreements also contain a requirement that tenants inform landlords as soon as reasonably possible if any repairs are needed; failure to do so could put you in breach.

✓If, one day, your landlord takes action against you (for example for the non-payment of rent), you may be able to use the fact that you are living in poor or unfit housing conditions as the basis of a 'counterclaim', which may reduce the amount you are required to pay.

✓Your landlord has to give you at least 24 hours' notice if they wish to access your property to inspect it or carry out repairs. They must also visit at a reasonable time of the day. The position is different if it is an emergency situation where immediate access is required.

Landlord harassment

You used to binge-watch TV shows about dodgy landlords and the awful things they would do to their tenants. You used to think, 'I'd never get myself into that situation.' But, here you are, in that very situation …

Landlord bad behaviour can range from the simply annoying to things that might qualify as actual harassment. Just because they own the property does not mean they have the right to abuse their power, and it is worth you knowing your available options. You might be being harassed by your landlord if, for example, they are trying to disrupt your life and ability to enjoy your home, trying to make you leave the property, or are making you feel unsafe in the property. Examples of specific behaviours may include the landlord doing the following:

- entering the property without your permission
- sending builders round without notice
- stopping you from having guests
- turning off your energy supplies
- being violent or abusive

If it is possible (and safe to do so), the quickest way to resolve the issue may be to write to your landlord telling them to stop their problematic behaviour. You could inform them that you intend to take legal action if the problem persists.

If your landlord does not stop despite you asking them to, you may wish to consider:

- contacting the police
- asking the council to step in and assist you (if your

council has a tenancy relations officer, ask to speak to this person)

- seeking legal advice: you may be able to obtain an injunction to stop the problematic behaviour

The housing charities listed in the Useful Organisations section at the back of the book (p. 277) will be able to assist further.

In some cases, harassment may lead to *illegal eviction* – we'll talk more about that towards the end of this chapter.

✓Wherever possible, keep a record of the harassment. It will bolster the strength of your case if you decide to take legal action.

Neighbour disputes

There are a number of reasons why neighbours may find themselves in a dispute. A knowledge of the law on some of the most common neighbour disputes may provide you with extra vim for when you are arguing (or, alternatively, encourage you to let them have the victory – this time). **To be as helpful as possible, this section isn't just for those who have neighbour disputes at the property they are renting, but also for homeowners in the same situation.**

General tips

Speak to the neighbour directly. If you find yourself in a neighbour dispute, it is often best to start by having a straightforward conversation with them. If you are hesitant to approach them, you could write a note explaining the problem and put it through their letter box, or even put it in the post if you don't want to go near their premises. If the problem is affecting other neighbours, you could band together and write a joint note. This may put additional pressure on the neighbour to stop their problematic behaviour.

Speak to your neighbour's landlord. If you've been complaining for a while without seeing any difference, you may want to up the ante by making a complaint to your neighbour's landlord (if they are living in a rented property). As a general rule, having a good relationship with the landlord of the house next door is advisable. Often the landlord of the house next door will *want* you to have their contact details, as they will see you as somebody able to keep a watchful eye over their property. The benefit to you is that you have a direct line to them if there are ever any serious issues.

Contact a mediator. If a problem is irritating you to the extent that you are considering legal action, you may first wish to contact a mediator. Mediators are individuals trained in assisting people in resolving disputes. Their services will usually be much cheaper than taking legal action to resolve a problem. Nonetheless, mediation will only be an option if your problematic neighbour is actually willing to engage in it, which won't always be the case. More information on mediation can be found on p. 266.

How to deal with the most common neighbour disputes

My neighbour is noisy! If you can, it's best to start by simply asking them to keep it down. If this does not work, you can contact the council. Many local councils provide an online form allowing you to detail your noise complaint, from which they can start investigating the incident – or you could give them a ring, if that's easier for you. You could also contact your neighbour's landlord detailing the problem.

My neighbour's hedges are too high! The first step, if possible, is to have a chat with your neighbour about the issue. The council will reject your complaint if it does not think you have taken reasonable steps to sort out the issue before involving it. There is a lot of guidance about the rules on high hedges online; google 'high hedges complaining to the council' and click the gov.uk link. Among other factors, the council is only likely to look into your complaint if the hedges are more than two metres high and are therefore affecting your enjoyment of your home or garden.

My neighbour wants me to pay to repair our shared broken fence! Sometimes a wall or fence that may appear to be shared will actually be owned by either yourself or your neighbour depending on where the boundary between your homes lies. To figure out where the boundary is, check the legal documents you will have received when you bought the home. If you don't have these documents, they can be obtained from the Land Registry for a small fee. Google 'property search land registry' and click either the gov.uk or Land Registry link. Within a few clicks you will reach a page where you can enter your address and obtain the documents. Where it is not clear from the documents who owns the fence, many neighbours choose to split the cost.

If your neighbour wishes to do something to a wall or fence they share with you, they should give you notice first (and vice versa). When wanting to do things to shared walls or fences, it's best to have a chat with your neighbour and see if an agreement can be reached. Compromise often tends to be the best way forward.

My neighbour's fence is driving me up the wall! It might be the case that you feel your neighbour's wall or fence is too low, meaning you do not have any privacy. It might be that it is a horrible colour and doesn't match the colour scheme of your garden. You cannot make your neighbour change their wall or fence just because it would better suit you. You also can't paint your side of it without their permission, even if you are pretty sure they would never realise. If you think your neighbour's wall or fence is dangerous, you can report it to the council. It is a good idea to speak to your neighbour first if you can though, as they may be happy to fix it if they are alerted to the issue.

My neighbour is harassing me/being abusive! If, having exhausted all attempts at resolving a dispute through polite conversation, your neighbour's behaviour develops into harassment or abuse, the most appropriate route would be to call the police. The same goes for if your neighbour is breaking the law (or you suspect them to be) in any other way.

✓ It is a good idea to know if the thing you are complaining about is a 'statutory nuisance'. Search the term on Google. The council has a *duty* to investigate these – giving you a stronger leg to stand on. Statutory nuisances include issues relating to certain noise complaints, artificial lights, a build-up of rubbish that could be harmful to health, smoke coming from premises, and smells and insects from business premises. You can quote the Environmental Protection Act 1990 in your correspondence with the council. Remember: whether you are complaining about an issue to the council, to a landlord, or to a neighbour directly – it is a good idea to have evidence.

Deposits

With a few days left of your tenancy, you decide to host a leaving party. News spreads more widely than you'd expected: fifty people turn up, and more keep coming, bottles in hand, all ready to have a good time. 'Let's make this a party to remember!' you hear one scream, and the others cheer back in approval. With your head in your hands, you realise the trip to Paris you had planned upon return of your deposit won't be happening after all. You hadn't previously given much thought to your deposit; you'd just assumed you'd get it back. Now you're not so sure. But this isn't the only way to lose a deposit ...

What is a deposit?

A deposit is a sum of money paid to your landlord when your tenancy starts. It is intended to give the landlord some security. If when you leave the property there is damage, or perhaps outstanding rent payments, maybe items missing, or perhaps the house is very dirty and will require a thorough clean, the landlord can keep all or part of your deposit to recoup their losses. If these issues do not apply, you *absolutely* should get your deposit back. 'Reasonable wear and tear' is not a reason for your landlord to take money from your deposit. This means that if your carpet looks a little more worn than it was when you first moved in (you know, because you walked on it …), you shouldn't have deductions taken from your deposit on this basis.

What's the maximum deposit amount I can be asked to provide?

If your total annual rent is less than £50,000, the deposit cannot be more than 5 weeks' rent. If the annual rent is £50,000 or more, the deposit cannot be more than 6 weeks' rent.

You can calculate the maximum deposit amount with this calculation:

Your monthly rent $\times$ 12 $\div$ 52 $\times$ 5* = maximum tenancy deposit
     * or 6, depending on the annual rent, as explained above.

Protection of deposits

When you pay your landlord the deposit, they have 30 days to 'protect' it. Depending on which deposit protection scheme your landlord uses (more on the different schemes later), this will involve either the money being taken from the landlord and held by the deposit protection scheme themselves, or your landlord keeping hold of the money but paying an insurance fee to the deposit protection scheme.

Your deposit being protected can give you some confidence that it isn't funding your landlord's 'Tenerife with the kids' summer getaway.

Your landlord should give you written confirmation of the deposit's protection within 30 days. This is known as the 'prescribed information' and is set out in the Housing (Tenancy Deposits) (Prescribed Information) Order 2007, which is worth taking a look at. Among other details, it requires your landlord to give you information stating:

- the amount of the deposit
- the name, address and contact details of the tenancy deposit protection scheme administrator
- the address of the property
- the name, address and contact details of the landlord and the tenant

How to check if your deposit is protected

Your landlord is required to inform you of the name of the

protection scheme protecting your deposit. Therefore, if you are in a position where you need to check in the first place, something has probably gone wrong. Asking your landlord might jog their memory (either to tell you, or put your deposit in the scheme, or both!).

To check if your deposit is protected, go to the website of each of the three deposit protection scheme providers. You will be required to enter your surname, postcode, tenancy start date and deposit amount. If the website you are on is that of the deposit scheme protecting your deposit, you will be alerted to this. The three deposit protection scheme providers are:

- Deposit Protection Service (depositprotection.com)
- MyDeposits (mydeposits.co.uk)
- Tenancy Deposit Scheme (tenancydepositscheme.com)

Failure to protect your deposit

If upon reading this you realise that your landlord failed to protect your deposit, rest assured that you are still entitled to get it back when you leave.

It is worth knowing that a landlord failing to follow the rules when you paid your deposit is taken very seriously. Even if you get your full deposit back, if you have the inclination, you could go to court and potentially obtain compensation of 1–3 times the amount of the deposit if your landlord:

- failed to protect your deposit within 30 days of receiving it
- failed to protect your deposit at all
- failed to give you the written information about the property and your deposit within 30 days
- failed to give you this written information at all

It is a good idea to gather as much evidence as you can – including proof you paid the deposit and any evidence you can find that the rules were not followed.

✓ Let's say you are a joint tenant. The deposit scheme requires that one individual be the lead tenant. In such a situation, it is the lead tenant who will be responsible for receiving all of the documents relating to the deposit scheme. That person will act on behalf of all of you when dealing with the deposit scheme. Make it the responsible one in the group. The one who remembers birthdays and never misses a train.

✓ Leaving a property, especially if it is on bad terms, can be very distressing. You have 6 years to claim compensation if your landlord failed to follow tenancy deposit protection rules. Therefore, feel free to wait a while and blow off some steam before picking up your battle-axe. Just make sure that you don't lose valuable evidence in the meantime!

Deductions from your deposit

Landlords must tell you why they are deducting money from your deposit amount. Get them to put their reasons in writing so that if you want to make a complaint, it is easier to do.

Get as much specific information as you can. For example, if they say they needed to repaint the wall, get them to send you a quote for the cost of having done this so you know that the amount being taken out of your deposit is fair. If they are trying to use the two small scuff marks you left on the bottom of the wall as the basis for redecorating the whole room and taking the cost of this out of your deposit, this is something you could challenge through the Alternative Dispute Resolution service provided by the deposit protection schemes (more on this later).

Inventory

When you start your tenancy, often your landlord or letting agent will provide you with an inventory. This will state the condition of the property when you moved in and you will be asked to sign it. It might say, for example, 'There is a dent on the left side of the wardrobe.' When the tenancy ends, your landlord will know it wasn't you that caused the dent and will not take the money to repair it out of your deposit.

When you receive the inventory from your landlord or letting agent, you should check the property yourself to make sure everything is as described on the inventory. If there is also a dent on the right side of the wardrobe, you should note this down on the inventory before you sign it. This means you will not be blamed for this dent when you are ready to move out. If there is anything that is a little tricky to explain, snap a photo of it and attach it to the inventory.

It is not a legal requirement for your landlord to provide you with an inventory; however, it is in both your interests that an inventory exists. Therefore, if you have not been provided with one, you may wish to draw up an inventory of your own, carefully noting down the condition of the property. You can then request that your landlord sign it, evidencing their agreement. If your landlord refuses to sign it, you can ask an independent inventory clerk to produce an inventory – but this will cost.

Alternative Dispute Resolution

If, despite your best efforts, you still can't agree with your landlord on how much of your deposit should be taken, you may wish to consider using your deposit protection scheme's Alternative Dispute Resolution (ADR) service. This is a free service and it is a condition of the deposit protection scheme that your landlord engage with the service in the event of a dispute. As part of the ADR service, your landlord will be asked to provide evidence supporting their argument on why the said amount of deduction to the deposit should be made. You will then have the opportunity to respond to this, detailing why you don't agree with the landlord's proposed deductions. In order to give yourself the best chance of getting the correct amount of money back, utilise the fact that you can upload attachments to your response. Attach as much as you can to support your case. For example, if the landlord is arguing that the house was left in a dirty condition, attach your own photos showing how tidy the house was when you left it, or the receipts from when you paid a cleaner to clean the property before you left. If the landlord is complaining about damage to the property that you had in fact reported to them, but which became worse over time because they failed to deal with the issue, attach screenshots of the texts where you were complaining about the issue. (ADR can be used in lots of other contexts too – see Chapter 12, on the justice system, for more information.)

✓ It is sensible to always prepare as if you are going to have an issue getting your deposit back. Therefore, whenever you correspond with your landlord via text or take pictures of your property, imagine that one day you will need to be attaching those pieces of evidence to an ADR form. Don't just keep the photos or texts on your phone, but also save them to the cloud and email a copy of the texts to yourself. With deposits frequently amounting to hundreds of pounds, it makes no sense losing this money simply because you dropped your iPhone in the bath and hadn't backed up vital evidence supporting your case.

Eviction

You're renting the perfect property. It's close to your workplace, you have friends in the area, but most importantly, it's kitted out so it truly feels like your home. For a reason unknown to you, your landlord takes a dislike to you (hopefully not just because of the Arsenal flag in the window). One day you receive a letter out of the blue. Its wording is a little cryptic, but you get the sense that your landlord is thinking of evicting you.

Before any eviction, your landlord needs to provide you with a 'notice'. There are two types of eviction: eviction following a Section 8 notice and eviction following a Section 21 notice. What do these mean?

- A Section 8 notice is what might be called a 'fault eviction' (i.e. the landlord feels you've done something wrong).
- A Section 21 notice is what might be called a 'no fault eviction' (i.e. the landlord doesn't need to think you've done something wrong).

The notice is the first step a landlord must take in an effort to evict you. The notice must contain particular information to be legally valid, and therefore will have a formal appearance.

Section 8 eviction

When a landlord wants you to leave the property for a reason that, by law, would entitle them to have their property back, the landlord will write and provide you with a Section 8 notice. As is the case for a Section 21 notice, the notice must contain particular information to be legally valid, and therefore will have a formal appearance. These legal reasons are called 'grounds': they include rent arrears, damage to the property, nuisance and antisocial behaviour.

The most common use of the Section 8 notice is under

Ground 8 which is where at least 2 months' rent is owed (however, any amount of arrears, even if less than 2 months, can be the subject of a notice under Ground 10). The Section 8 notice will read at the top: *'Notice seeking possession'*. It will tell you what legal ground your landlord is relying on and at what date they will be able to apply to the court for 'possession' of the property (i.e. apply to the court asking it to make an 'order' that the landlord possess the house again) if you have not already left.

The amount of time the law allows between you receiving the notice and the landlord being able to go to court depends on the ground they are relying on. When the Section 8 notice is due to the non-payment of at least 2 months' rent, it is 2 weeks' notice.

The landlord will hope that receiving the Section 8 notice triggers you to pay the rent arrears or leave the property of your own accord, but if you don't, matters may proceed to court.

If the matter proceeds to court, it is worth knowing that there are two categories of legal ground your landlord can rely on. These are 'mandatory grounds' and 'discretionary grounds'.

Mandatory grounds mean the judge *must* make an order enabling the landlord to have their property back if they are able to prove the existence of the ground. The most commonly used mandatory ground is Ground 8 – this is where you owe at least 2 months' rent (as mentioned earlier).

Discretionary grounds are grounds where the court may still let you stay in your home if it believes it reasonable to do so. Breach of tenancy obligation is an example of a discretionary ground. So, for example, having pets when your tenancy agreement states that you cannot.

When the landlord makes their application to the court for possession of the property (due to the fact that you haven't moved out), the court will send you a form to fill out for your defence, as well as a copy of the claim form the landlord sent to the court. Fill in your form as thoroughly as possible, explaining how you may be able to rectify the situation (e.g. how you intend to pay the backlog of rent), and, if appropriate, detailing whether or not the landlord's claims are even true!

There will then be a court hearing where you can put across your side of the story. Arrive early and, if you don't have a lawyer, make use of the 'duty adviser' who can give you free legal advice before your hearing and even represent you.

If the landlord cannot prove that you have breached the legal ground they are relying on, their claim will be dismissed. If the landlord can prove it, the judge will either make something called an 'outright possession order', where the court will state the date by which you will need to move out; or, they may make a possession order but 'suspend' it (a suspended possession order can only be made on a discretionary ground, so is not available in relation to, for example, Ground

8). This means that you can stay in the property *provided* you keep to certain conditions as stated by the court. This might include keeping up with a certain level of repayments.

If you do not keep to the conditions the court told you to in a suspended possession order, or you stay in the property after the date the court told you to leave in an outright possession order, then the landlord can apply to the court for 'enforcement agents' to evict you (enforcement agents were previously, and sometimes still are, referred to as 'bailiffs').

✓It is worth seeking legal advice if you are at risk of eviction. Even on mandatory grounds, there may be legal arguments that can be made that persuade a court not to make a court order resulting in your eviction.

Section 21 eviction

A Section 21 notice is the notice the landlord must give you if they wish to get their property back without providing a legal reason for doing so. This is appropriate in circumstances where there isn't actually anything you've done wrong (e.g. not paying your rent).

For a Section 21 notice, your landlord must give you 2 months' notice. In practice this means that, if the landlord writes to you on 7 June stating they want you to leave by 7 August, and you haven't left by this date, your landlord can apply to the court for a possession order.

Once the landlord has applied to the court, the court will send you papers for you to write a defence – in other words, why you want to challenge the eviction. This book has insufficient space to detail the numerous potential ways of challenging your Section 21 notice, but the following resources may assist:

- 'Guidance – Understanding the possession action process: A guide for private residential tenants in England and Wales' (at gov.uk)
- 'Shelter: Restrictions on use of section 21 for assured shorthold tenancies' (at england.shelter.org.uk)

A Google search using those terms will bring both websites up.

The court will make a decision as to whether a court hearing is needed (i.e. a date when both you and the landlord can attend court to make arguments in front of a judge). If you don't return your defence, or your arguments are not strong enough, the court could grant the landlord the possession order they applied for and order you to leave the property without there being a court hearing.

The court will usually give you 2 weeks to leave the property. This date will be clearly stated on the possession order.

If you don't leave by the date the court states, the landlord can apply to the court for enforcement agents (bailiffs) to evict you.

✓ Your landlord loses the ability to apply for a possession order if they wait longer than 12 months from when they gave you your Section 8 notice, or 6 months from when they gave you your Section 21 notice. Let's say that you are given a Section 21 notice on 7 June which rightfully gives you your 2 months' notice, stating you are to leave the property by 7 August. If you do not leave and your landlord doesn't make an issue of this, the landlord cannot then use that notice to apply to the court for a possession order two years later (... although they can of course serve a fresh notice at that later time).

✓ A far wiser barrister than I once told me, 'In housing law, nothing is static.' Even if you hadn't paid 2 months' rent when the landlord gave you the Section 8 notice, if you no longer owe as much as 2 months' rent by the date of the hearing, the landlord can't continue to rely on the ground. Likewise, if by the time of the hearing the antisocial behaviour problems the landlord has spoken of seem to have ceased (e.g. perhaps the friend who used to come round and cause all the noise has moved abroad), the court may decide it wouldn't be reasonable to kick you out.

✓ Eviction notices must be 'valid'. If they are not valid – they don't count. A notice might be invalid if it doesn't provide a date for you to leave the property, or the date provided does not give you the amount of notice you are legally entitled to. A Section 8 notice might be invalid if it doesn't explain which specific ground is being used to evict you. Our homes are one of the most important things in our lives. If you are given a court hearing to defend your case, although you may feel it a waste of time, just turning up and setting out your circumstances can often make a difference. It allows the judge to hear not only your landlord's side of the argument, but yours too.

Illegal eviction

If a landlord takes action to deprive you of access to all or

part of the premises without following the correct legal procedures, this amounts to an illegal eviction. (This applies not
just to a landlord but in fact to *any person* taking such action,
and as such, for the rest of this section, 'the landlord' should
be understood to encompass any such individual.)

Examples of ways illegal evictions can be carried out
include:

- changing the locks while you are out
- blocking access to part of the premises, e.g. locking the
  door to the kitchen
- using force to physically remove you

An illegal eviction is not necessarily permanent. You may
be illegally evicted for just a few days – for example if the
locks were changed while you were out, but then after angry
calls to your landlord you are allowed back in a few days
later. Even if this is the case, this still counts as an illegal eviction and you may wish to consider legal action. It is worth
knowing that if you are illegally evicted and you act quickly,
you may be able to obtain an injunction requiring the landlord to allow you back into the accommodation, as well as
compensation.

If you don't take action at the time, but later downstream
your landlord takes action against you (for example for the
non-payment of rent), you may be able to use the historic
illegal eviction as a 'counterclaim', which may reduce the
amount the court requires you to pay back.

Harassment and illegal eviction are also criminal offences under Section 1 of the Protection from Eviction Act 1977. If your local authority has a tenancy relations service, the tenancy relations officer may investigate and threaten prosecution if the landlord fails to allow you back in immediately.

Your landlord will have a defence to the illegal eviction if they can show that they believed, or had reasonable cause to believe, that you were no longer residing in the property. This is the 'I thought she'd packed her bags and moved back in with her parents' defence. Whether the landlord will succeed with this defence will depend on all of the facts of the case.

It is a good idea to seek legal advice if you want to take your landlord to court for illegal eviction.

Enforcement agents (bailiffs) visiting your home

Enforcement agents visiting your home in order to evict you can feel horrible. Here are some things to know:

- Your notice of eviction will tell you the date and time the enforcement agents will be attending. If you fear you will be homeless when evicted, inform your local council from *now*. Do not wait until your eviction day.
- When they arrive, ask to see the warrant or 'writ of possession'. This is the document that gives the enforcement agents authority to evict.
- Be ready to leave when they arrive, as you will have limited (if any) time to pack your belongings.

- Unless there is a court order stating otherwise, enforcement agents cannot keep hold of your belongings to pay for your rent arrears or court costs.
- If belongings are left behind, your landlord must keep them safe for a reasonable period of time. The landlord can lawfully dispose of them after giving you a reasonable opportunity to collect them. Failure to collect the items could lead to you being charged for the costs of removal or storage. It is in your interest to contact the landlord and get your belongings back as soon as possible: possessions that are left behind after an eviction all too often go missing.

Disconnection of energy supply

Life isn't cheap. When times get really hard, we may find it difficult to pay for our energy bills. This can be particularly worrying alongside everything else going on. But there are protections you have, and it is important you know what these are so that you can rely on them if necessary.

Key things to know

The disconnection of your energy supply should always be a last resort by your energy provider. If you have been contacted by your supplier in relation to the disconnection of your supply, it is important to know that before any disconnection can take place, you must be given the chance to repay the money you owe through a range of options, including a payment plan. When discussing the idea of a payment plan with you, suppliers must take into account your financial circumstances and must only request you repay your energy debt in amounts that are realistic and sustainable for you.

Restrictions on who can be disconnected

Pensioners, disabled or chronically sick

Suppliers cannot disconnect premises occupied solely by pensioners (or if they also live with children under age 18) during the 'Winter Moratorium' (1 October – 31 March inclusive). Suppliers must also take all reasonable steps to avoid disconnecting premises that include any pensioners, disabled or chronically sick customers during the Winter Moratorium.

'Vulnerable customers'

If your energy supplier has signed up to the Vulnerability Commitment, they have pledged to never knowingly disconnect a vulnerable customer at any time of the year where the household has children under age 6 (or under age 16 during the Winter Moratorium) or where, for reasons of age, health, disability or severe financial insecurity, that customer is unable to safeguard their personal welfare or the personal welfare of other members of the household.

To see if your energy supplier is signed up to the Vulnerability Commitment, google 'vulnerability commitment Energy UK' where you will find more information.

Ofgem define vulnerability as: when a consumer's personal circumstances and characteristics combine with aspects of the market to create situations where he or she is:

- significantly less able than a typical domestic consumer to protect or represent their interests in the energy market; and/or
- significantly more likely than a typical domestic consumer to suffer detriment, or that detriment is likely to be more substantial.

(The term 'typical domestic consumer' simply refers to a customer living in this country, as opposed to in another one.)

Other occasions when you cannot be disconnected

You also cannot be disconnected if:

- your debt is owed to a previous supplier
- you have been made bankrupt and the debt relates to a period before you went bankrupt
- the debt is not for the gas or electricity you have used but for some other service or appliance you have bought from your supplier (such as a boiler or boiler service contract)

Prepayment meters

Instead of disconnection, it is likely that your energy supplier will ask to install a prepayment meter at your home. They can only install a prepayment meter if it would be 'safe and reasonably practicable' to do so (for example, they couldn't install it in a location that is not accessible to you, such as so high on a wall that you can't reach it). A prepayment meter is like having a 'top up'/'pay-as-you-go' phone. The more money you 'top it up' with, the longer it will last (in this case, the longer your energy will last). It is worth knowing that suppliers are also required to offer emergency support to customers struggling to top up their prepayment meter.

Suppliers may obtain a warrant to install a prepayment meter at your home, but only if they have been unsuccessful in first taking all other appropriate and proportionate steps to engage with you. Obtaining a warrant to install a prepayment meter must only be done as a last resort to avoid disconnecting the customer.

✓ There is a ban on using warrants to install a prepayment meter if a consumer would find the experience traumatic. Your supplier can ask you to pay charges in relation to the installation of the prepayment meter, but this is capped (£150 is the cap at the time of writing).

How is my supply physically disconnected?

The energy supplier can apply to the court for a warrant to enter your home and disconnect your energy supply if you cannot reach an agreement with them to pay off your debt. They cannot apply to the court behind your back – they must notify you first that that is what they will be doing.

There will be a court hearing where it will be decided whether the energy supplier is to be granted the warrant to enter your home to disconnect your energy supply. It is a good idea to attend this court hearing so you can make your voice heard.

It is important to remember that you can continue trying to come to an agreement regarding the paying off of your debt (perhaps the promise of monthly payments) with your energy supplier right up until the court makes their decision about the warrant. Therefore, before the hearing, contact your supplier to see if you can come to an agreement. Even at court itself, speak to the individual representing the energy supplier to see if an agreement can be reached.

If your energy meter is on the outside of your property, your supplier technically will not need a warrant to disconnect your supply, as the purpose of the warrant is to *enter* your property. Nonetheless, it is common practice for the energy supplier to still get a warrant.

If you have a smart meter, suppliers are able to disconnect your energy supply remotely; however, all other existing rules surrounding debt management continue to apply.

To get reconnected after a disconnection, contact your supplier. There may be costs and charges involved.

✓If you experience temporary disconnection because of a power cut, dial 105, the free power cut line, or visit powercut105.com. You might be due compensation from your network operator.

2

Relationships

Brits have a reputation for keeping all things private when it comes to relationships. While there is nothing wrong with this, it can lead to a knowledge void when it comes to exerting our rights in a relationship, and also puts us on the back foot when it comes to utilising our legal protections if something goes wrong. As with any relationship, some things are a matter of negotiation – you might think it's your right to choose tonight's film if your partner picked yesterday's, but they might well disagree. Other things are non-negotiable and falling foul of them is illegal.

Regardless of your sexuality, gender or marital status, the law offers you protections. This chapter will lay out the key bits of law you ought to know, whether you are in the love-struck early days of a new relationship, the comfortable space of a long-term relationship, or going through a relationship breakdown. It also seeks to answer the questions you probably wouldn't google (or even know to google), from the laws on 'sexting', or sending 'nudes', to the protections that exist if you are harassed or stalked by a partner or an ex.

It will also seek to myth bust. A 2018 YouGov survey commissioned by End Violence Against Women revealed that 'a third (33 per cent) of people in Britain think it isn't usually rape if a woman is pressured into having sex but there is no physical violence'. In addition, almost a quarter (24 per cent) of those surveyed believed 'in most cases it isn't rape if non-consensual sex occurs within a long-term relationship'. As this chapter will show, neither of these beliefs are true. While matters of consent are usually restricted to conversations concerning the act of rape, the absence of consent before embarking on sexual activity can make an individual fall foul of a number of other sexual offences too. This chapter will explore these issues.

Sexual consent

Consent is the fundamental tenet of any sexual relationship. But what exactly, in law, does it mean? This section will explore the world of consent, referencing Acts of Parliament, quotes from judges and factual examples. It will explain what consent *is* and what consent *is not*. It will also examine the law when different factors have been at play, for example, intoxication. No two cases are the same and, as such, it would be impossible to account for every eventuality. Nonetheless, it is hoped that having read this section, you will have an enhanced understanding of sexual consent.

What is the definition of 'consent'?

Section 74 of the Sexual Offences Act 2003 defines 'consent' as follows:

> A person consents if he agrees by choice, and has the freedom and capacity to make that choice.

(Note: legislation often uses male pronouns despite the words applying to everybody regardless of sex. This is such an example.)

The concepts of 'choice', 'freedom to make the choice' and 'capacity to make the choice' are of vital importance. The three cases below provide practical examples, respectively, of what these three concepts mean.

Case 1: **R(F) v DPP***

A woman consented to sexual intercourse on the clear understanding that the man would not ejaculate inside her vagina. When the man deliberately ejaculated inside her vagina, he did something to which she had not consented. Her consent was therefore negated. This meant his actions fell within the statutory definition of rape. She had been **deprived of choice** relating to the crucial element on which the original consent was based. (There is case law to the effect that consent based on the understanding the man wears a condom could be treated the same way.)

---

* [2013] EWHC 945 (Admin)

Case 2: **R v McNally**[*]

This was a case in which deception as to gender vitiated (impaired the legal validity of) the consent to sexual activity. A woman was made to think she was engaging in sexual activity with a male, but the individual was biologically female. The court said as follows:

> Thus while, in a physical sense, the acts of assault by penetration of the vagina are the same whether perpetrated by a male or a female, the sexual nature of the acts is, on any common sense view, different where the complainant is **deliberately deceived** by a defendant into believing the latter is a male. Assuming the facts to be proved as alleged, M **chose** to have sexual encounters with a boy and her preference (her **freedom** to choose whether or not to have a sexual encounter with a girl) was removed by the defendant's deception.

Case 3: **R v Bree**[†]

After spending an evening together and consuming considerable quantities of alcohol, a man and woman went back to the woman's flat, where they had sex. At court, the woman stated that she had not consented to the sexual intercourse that took place, and the man stated that he reasonably believed that she had consented.

---

* [2013] EWCA Crim 1051
† [2007] EWCA Crim 804

Three principles came out of this case:

1. If the effect of the alcohol was such that the individual temporarily **lost the capacity** to choose whether to engage in sexual activity, there will not have been consent.
2. If an individual voluntarily consumed substantial quantities of alcohol, but nevertheless **remained capable of choosing** whether to have intercourse, and agreed to do so, that would not be rape (and by extension, there would have been consent).
3. **Capacity to consent** may disappear well before a complainant becomes unconscious. Whether or not this is so will depend on the facts of the case.

When it comes to consent, what we learn from these cases is just how important it is to respect others' choices, preferences and conditions; and, of course, the importance of the person being in a position to be able to make such choices.

Consent, once given, is not unchanging – it can be withdrawn at any time, and can be negated if the terms on which it was given (e.g. the wearing of a condom) are not adhered to by the other party. Regretting sex having previously agreed to it does not mean the consent at the time was invalid.

Consent and 'reasonable belief'

You must have a 'reasonable belief' that the person has consented to sexual activity.

In determining whether your belief is reasonable, all

of the circumstances will be taken into account, including any steps you took to ascertain whether in fact the person consented.

The application of the reasonable belief principle can be explained as follows. For the purposes of the example, Person A is the person accused of the sexual offence and Person B is the complainant.

If Person A believed he had been given consent, but this belief was shown to be *unreasonably* held, then he would be guilty of the sexual offence. In contrast, Person A would *not* be guilty of the sexual offence if he *reasonably* believed, even if in error, that there was consent.

The following two questions can be asked to determine whether a belief was reasonable:

1. Did the defendant believe the complainant consented?
2. If the defendant did believe consent was given, was this a reasonable belief to have?

In reality, that might mean: did you ask for consent? Did you hear the other person say 'yes'? What other signs were given? If you believe you were given consent, what are you basing your belief on? In many circumstances, a person's voluntary and clear agreement to have sex will be the clearest way to have 'reasonable belief'.

Ages and consent

A person cannot legally consent to sexual activity before

the age of 16 (note: not just sexual intercourse, but sexual activity). Therefore, if anybody has any sexual activity with somebody under the age of 16, they break the law – that is even if both parties are under 16. Notwithstanding this, the intention of the law is to protect children, and not to prosecute those under 16 who mutually agree to sexual activity.

It is important to also note that if a person is aged 18 or over and holds certain positions of trust or authority in the life of somebody under the age of 18 (for example, they are a social worker, teacher or doctor), they break the law if they have any sexual activity with that person. This means that an 18-year-old teaching assistant could not engage in sexual activity with a 17-year-old studying at the college, despite the fact they are both over 16. It will be a defence if the two individuals are married (or in a civil partnership), or if a sexual relationship existed immediately before the position of trust arose.

Addressing misconceptions

Having provided clarity on the meaning of 'consent', it is important to tackle misconceptions people frequently have when it comes to sexual offences.

Rape is where:

- Person A intentionally penetrates the vagina, anus or mouth of Person B with his penis,

- without Person B's consent, and
- Person A does not reasonably believe that Person B consents.

This is the full legal definition of rape, and it can happen in any context. Just because two people are married does not, legally, mean the man is not able to rape his wife (or his husband). Because the act of rape requires penile penetration, it can only be committed by a man.

Assault by penetration is where:

- Person A penetrates the vagina or anus of Person B with a part of their body or anything else,
- the penetration is sexual,
- without Person B's consent, and
- Person A does not reasonably believe that Person B consents.

This offence can be committed by a person of any gender.

The penetration could be by any part of a person's body, such as their tongue, finger or toe, or anything else, such as a sex toy or household object. If the penetration is by a person's penis, this is rape. Unlike in rape, penetration of the mouth is not included.

Sexual assault is where:

- Person A touches Person B with sexual intent,

- Person B does not consent, and
- Person A does not reasonably believe Person B consents.

This offence can be committed by a person of any gender.

Touching through clothes in some circumstances can amount to sexual assault. The touching can be with any part of the body (so, not just necessarily a hand), or with anything else, such as an object, as long as the touching is sexual.

Domestic abuse

Recent statistics estimate that 2.3 million adults aged between 16 and 74 in England and Wales experienced domestic abuse in the course of one year.* That's roughly double the population of Birmingham.

This section could help save somebody's life. Domestic abuse is massively under-reported, and it affects people regardless of class, education, age or race. People may also keep what is happening to them private out of shame. If you or somebody you know finds themselves in a domestically abusive situation, you may wonder what protections are available. Something that can make this a tricky area to address is that many don't know what 'counts' as domestic abuse and may not appreciate that it may include things that

---

* https://www.ons.gov.uk/peoplepopulationandcommunity/
crimeandjustice/bulletins/domesticabuseinenglandandwalesoverview/
november2020

they are facing. This section will be split into dealing with the offences that can come under domestic abuse, and then setting out the legal protections that exist.

What is the definition of 'domestic abuse'?

Contrary to common belief, 'domestic abuse' is not the name of a specific offence. The definition of domestic abuse presently used by the government (not a legal definition) is as follows:

> Any incident or pattern of incidents of controlling, coercive or threatening behaviour, violence or abuse between those aged 16 or over who are or have been intimate partners or family members regardless of gender or sexuality. This can encompass but is not limited to the following types of abuse: psychological, physical, sexual, financial, or emotional.

There are a number of different offences that, depending on their circumstances, could come under this definition. While violence and threats may be easier to spot at first instance, behaviour that is controlling and coercive is sometimes overlooked, despite very much being capable of constituting domestic abuse.

The offence of 'controlling or coercive behaviour in an intimate or family relationship' is a relatively new offence, coming into force in 2015.

This is a criminal offence committed by A, if:

- A repeatedly or continuously engages in behaviour towards another person (B) that is controlling or coercive; and
- at the time of the behaviour, A and B are personally connected; and
- the behaviour has a serious effect on B; and
- A knows or ought to know that the behaviour will have a serious effect on B.

A and B are 'personally connected', if:

- they are in an intimate personal relationship; or
- they live together and are members of the same family; or
- they live together and have previously been in an intimate personal relationship with each other.

Examples of controlling and coercive behaviour might include the individual repeatedly and/or continuously engaging in any of the following:

- isolating you from your friends
- monitoring your online communications
- humiliating you
- controlling your finances
- restricting your freedom to leave the house

A's behaviour has a 'serious effect' on B if:

- it causes B to fear, on at least two occasions, that violence will be used against B, or

- it causes B serious alarm or distress which has a substantial adverse effect on B's usual day-to-day activities.

What does this look like in practice?

Joe and Janine are in a relationship. From the moment Janine steps in the house, Joe demands that he has hold of her phone so that he can see any messages coming through. The couple recently had a baby and Joe will frequently criticise Janine's mothering and housekeeping skills. In his mind, the house is never clean enough and he calls her a 'trampy woman'. Janine is not allowed to go out the house without Joe first approving what she is wearing. If Joe is not in, Janine must send him a photo of what she is wearing. Janine also cannot buy anything for their baby unless Joe has first agreed that it is a suitable purchase. More and more Janine stops leaving the house, and the close connection she once had with her friends and wider family starts to erode.

This is an example that includes many coercive and controlling behaviours, and it has a substantial adverse effect on Janine's day-to-day activities. But you don't need to experience all of these behaviours for the perpetrator to have committed the offence – even just one behaviour, if it has happened continuously or repeatedly (more than once), could be sufficient.

It is important to know that if, say, an act of violence is committed in a domestic abuse context – for example, you are punched by your partner – your partner will be charged for the offence in the same way as would be the case if it were not done in a domestic abuse context. There is no specific offence for domestic-related violence. Nonetheless, the court is likely to treat the offence more seriously and pass a harsher sentence when presented with the fact that the victim of the offence was the perpetrator's partner.

Harassment and stalking

Harassment and stalking typically apply when you have a more limited (if any) relationship with the perpetrator. Nonetheless, it could equally apply to behaviour from an ex-partner whom you no longer live with.

Harassment

Harassment does not have a strict legal definition, but, as stated on the Crown Prosecution Service's website: '… can include repeated attempts to impose unwanted communications and contact upon a victim in a manner that could be expected to cause distress or fear in any reasonable person.'

Stalking

Stalking could be said to be a type of harassment but is a criminal offence in its own right.

There is not a strict legal definition of stalking; however, Section 2A(3) of the Protection from Harassment Act 1997 provides examples of things that, in particular circumstances, are associated with stalking. Examples given include following a person, watching or spying on a person, and contacting or attempting to contact a person by any means (which could include social media).

Protections

If you identify with any of the above, you may be wondering what your next step is.

The following section details some of the legal protections available to you. I must stress the importance of turning to the Useful Organisations section (p. 277) where you can find the details of organisations that work in this area, who will be able to give you personalised advice. Also be aware that your GP can be a gateway to domestic abuse support. This book cannot attempt to explore all the facets of an issue as complex as domestic abuse; the following serves only to give you an insight into the options available so that you can have a more informed conversation with the organisations. **Of course – if you are in immediate danger – call 999.**

The Domestic Violence Disclosure Scheme, or 'Clare's Law'

This enables you to request that the police inform you if the person you are in a relationship with may pose a risk of harm to you. It is known as the 'right to ask'. Family and close friends can also make enquiries about an individual if they are concerned they may pose a risk of harm to you. Don't worry though – if somebody (e.g. your friend Adeola) makes enquiries about your partner, the police will inform *you* that your partner is a potential risk, not them (Adeola).

The police may also decide to tell you your partner is a risk to you, even if you've never asked. This is called the 'right to know'.

Apply for a 'non-molestation order' under the Family Law Act 1996

A non-molestation order is a court order forbidding an abuser from certain actions. The court order might state, for example, that your abuser is not to contact you by social media, email, telephone, in person or via another person. It is an arrestable offence if this court order is breached.

Apply for a 'harassment injunction' under the Protection from Harassment Act 1997

A harassment injunction orders the person harassing you to stop their behaviour. If they do not, it is a criminal offence and they can be prosecuted.

Apply for an 'occupation order' under the Family Law Act 1996

An occupation order regulates the family home. For example, it may prevent your abuser from being able to live in the home, or from visiting your home and its surrounding area. If a power of arrest has been attached to the order, breach of it from your abuser can result in their arrest. If a power of arrest has not been attached and your abuser breaches the order, you would go back to court to commence contempt of court proceedings. If successful, these proceedings could result in the person being fined and/or sent to prison.

Domestic Violence Protection Notices (DVPNs) and Domestic Violence Protection Orders (DVPOs)

DVPNs and DVPOs can provide short-term protection to a victim.

A DVPN can be given by the police to your abuser if they have reasonable grounds for believing that your abuser has been violent or has threatened violence towards you, and that the DVPN is necessary to protect you. The obtaining of a DVPN will usually require you to have reported the issue to the police or them having become aware of the domestic violence in some other way. The DVPN may state that the perpetrator must leave your home, or is prohibited from coming within a certain distance of your home. If the DVPN is breached, the perpetrator will be arrested. The police have 48 hours from the time the DVPN is given to your abuser to apply for a DVPO. A DVPO is an order from the court. For the court to order a DVPO it must be satisfied that it is more likely than not that violence has been used or threatened towards you and that ordering the DVPO is necessary to protect you. A DVPO allows the prohibitions that were within the DVPN to continue for up to 28 days. This buys some time for the police to further their investigations, provides you with respite from your abuser and enables you to obtain assistance from support services without interference from the perpetrator.

Housing protections

If you need to leave your home urgently:

You may be able to get a place in a refuge. Contact the National Domestic Abuse Helpline who can talk you through your options (see p. 283) (or a service local to your area).

You could contact your local authority and ask for homelessness help. When speaking with the council, be as open as you can. Housing officers will have received training on how to deal with people in your situation, and should respond in a professional and sympathetic manner.

If the local authority has 'reason to believe' that you have suffered domestic abuse or are at risk of suffering domestic abuse, and you are eligible for assistance (in that you meet certain immigration status conditions), it will have a duty to provide you with emergency accommodation where you will be safe.

If you have children or other persons who usually live with you, the local authority must also accommodate them as members of your household.

During its enquiries into your homelessness application the local authority may seek information from your GP, the police, social services or your friends and relatives. It must ensure that its enquiries do not provoke further violence or abuse, and it should not approach the perpetrator.

You can apply to your own local authority for assistance. But if you think that you will not be safe anywhere in the district of your local authority, it is advisable to apply to a different local authority. That authority cannot refer you back to your 'own' authority if there is a risk of domestic abuse in that area.

✔ If you are living in the UK as a spouse, civil partner or unmarried partner of a British citizen or person settled in the UK, and domestic violence has led to your relationship ending, you may be able to apply for 'indefinite leave to remain' in the UK. The organisations listed in the back of the book will be able to provide more information.

✔ Various smartphone apps allow you to see the location of others. If you move out to get away from an abusive partner, or if you are being stalked, you may want to ensure you cannot be located through apps. Check the location and privacy settings on your mobile. Snapchat and Find my iPhone are two apps that can quite easily be used to locate somebody. Other social media sites may automatically post your location when you write a post or share a photo; be sure to turn these settings off. You may wish to download the app Hollie Guard, which can be used to raise an alert to trusted phone contacts if you feel unsafe.

✔ If you are in immediate danger, you should call 999. If you cannot speak or whisper (i.e. because your abuser is close), your call will be transferred to the Silent Solution team. You will hear an automated 20-second message that begins with the phrase 'you are through to the police'. You will then be asked to press '55' to be put through to police call management. Your call will be transferred to your local police force where you will be asked 'yes' or 'no' questions. If you are unable to speak, you will be given instructions (for example, told to press certain numbers) so that the call handler can communicate with you.

✓ The Domestic Abuse Act 2021, at the time of writing, is not yet in force. Nonetheless, it will change some of the information in this area. The organisations listed at the back of the book will be able to tell you what this means for you.

Sending or receiving explicit photos/'sexting', 'revenge porn' and 'upskirting'

Around 80 per cent of UK adults own a smartphone. Shockingly, 50 per cent of under-10s own one too. With such a large proportion of the population having a camera in their pocket, in conjunction with the rise of Snapchat, TikTok, dating apps – you name it – there is an increasing need for a better awareness of the law surrounding such matters as the sending and receiving of explicit photos. The consequences can be serious and some of the laws may not be obvious. This section aims to demystify.

Sending your 'nudes' – under 18

If you are under 18 and take and send a sexually explicit photo of yourself to somebody else, you technically have committed the offences of taking and distributing an indecent photograph of a child, contrary to Section 1 of the Protection of Children Act 1978. It does not matter that the photo is of you or that it's a selfie. The person you send the image to will then 'possess' the image, which also exposes them to criminal liability.

In practice, those under 18 are unlikely to be prosecuted for the consensual sending of images. Nonetheless, this is arguably an example of where the law will need to be reconsidered in the future. The Protection of Children Act came into force in 1978 and was intended to help prevent the exploitation of children, but the present situation is such that the Act can potentially criminalise the children it aims to protect.

Sending your 'nudes' – 18 or over

If you are 18 or over, taking and sending a sexually explicit photo of yourself is not against the law. Nonetheless, if you send the image and it is unwanted by the recipient (e.g. instances of 'cyber flashing' or sending an unsolicited 'dick pic'), you may be guilty of offences under the Malicious Communications Act 1988 or the Sexual Offences Act 2003, depending on the circumstances. Again, the law at the moment has not quite caught up with the issue of 'cyber flashing'. The Law Commission (a statutory body that make recommendations for consideration by Parliament) is currently investigating reform in this area – so change may be on the way.

'Revenge porn'

If you share a private sexual photograph or video without the consent of the person appearing in the photograph or video, with the intention of causing that individual distress, you have committed an offence. This issue has come to prominent attention in recent years with individuals sharing sexually explicit photos of ex-partners, often in what is called 'revenge porn'. You could receive up to 2 years' imprisonment.

'Upskirting'

'Upskirting' is when photographic equipment is placed at an angle to be able to see under somebody's clothing to take a voyeuristic photograph without their permission. It is not limited to victims wearing skirts, nor is it limited to women – the offence can also cover those wearing, for example, kilts, shorts, trousers and cassocks. You could receive up to 2 years' imprisonment.

3

Shopping

On average we are exposed to around 5,000 adverts per day, the vast majority of which encourage us to buy something. You can't walk down a street or open an internet browser without being sold something that – let's be honest – you probably don't need. But if it seems like the worst that might happen in a shop is that you buy something in a spontaneous and regrettable splurge, then think again.

There are a number of things retailers are required to do by law, but if the public are unaware of them, then retailers can get away with all sorts. Many of us trust that we'll get what we pay for, and that, since 'the customer is king', we'll be treated with fairness and respect. The reality is that this can be as foolish as clicking on a spam email link that promises incredible riches in exchange for your bank details. In other words: don't fall into the trap!

Equally, there are real positives to knowing your rights in this area – getting rid of the ugly jumper that doesn't fit you but you thought you couldn't take back is one. Or, how about

obtaining a full refund instead of an exchange when returning an item to a store that you, categorically, never intend to
shop at again.

This chapter won't just touch on conventional 'retail', but
also on products and services. It will let you know the law if
you go to the hairdresser who promises to use only '100 per
cent natural' products, but whose shampoo has an ingredients
list as convoluted as a Gmail automated password suggestion.
It will also give you the conviction to ask for a price reduction
when the professional window cleaner you hired makes no
real effort to, well, actually clean the windows.

All in all, the aim of this chapter is to give you confidence.
When something goes wrong, it is going to enable you to
say, 'Can I see the manager?' with a tad more assertiveness
in your voice. This time, you will be armed with a working
knowledge of the law, as opposed to just the sense that you've
been wronged.

Returning goods

Sometimes we buy things and realise that actually, for whatever reason, we want to return them. This section details all
the rights you have when returning a product. Some of the
information in this section is not well known at all. In fact,
many shop assistants themselves may not know these rights.
So, when talking to them, make sure you know exactly what
you're talking about – you could even show them this book!

Returning a pinstripe shirt (an example)

It's the week before the work Christmas party and you've bought a fancy new pinstripe shirt to show your pals how fashionable you are outside of your nine-to-five. Let's go through a couple of scenarios.

You look in the mirror and …

… realise the shirt is defective

(Or, to be more precise and quote the Consumer Rights Act 2015, realise the item is not: fit for purpose, as described, or of satisfactory quality.)

- You've got 30 days to return it and still be entitled to a full refund. This is irrespective of what the store's returns policy says. Don't be tricked into accepting an exchange when you could have had a full refund. (Note that this short-term right to reject the goods and obtain a full refund does not apply to perishable goods, such as fruit, where the 30-day returns period is reduced to the period within which the goods would ordinarily be expected to perish.)
- If you don't find the fault within the first 30 days, but find it within 6 months, you can still return the item. However, you will need to give the retailer a chance to fix the problem or offer you a replacement at least once. If they cannot do this, or if after one repair or replacement the issue remains, you can request a refund (which is called your final right to reject the goods).

- If you notice the fault after 6 months, the onus is on *you* to prove the fault was there when you purchased the goods, which is likely to be difficult. The law doesn't tell us exactly how we can do this, which is why it's so important to check for faults the moment you buy something – the more expensive an item is, the more important you check!

... think 'Damn – this is a horrible shirt. Why are shop mirrors so deceiving?'

- Even if the item isn't faulty, most shops have a returns policy, allowing you to return the item and get a refund, exchange or credit note. It is important to note that shops **do not legally have to have** a returns policy. But, if they do, they must abide by it.

Guarantees and warranties

What is a guarantee? A guarantee often comes free with a product. I recently purchased a vacuum cleaner that had on it a sticker from the manufacturer stating that if any defects occurred within 5 years, I could get a replacement. This sounds great, right? But don't necessarily allow this to sway your decision-making. Often, you will need to fill out a registration card and send it to the manufacturer, or log on to the manufacturer's website and fill in a registration form within a specified timeframe before your guarantee is 'validated'. The reality is that many people *don't* do this because they don't realise they have to or, alternatively, they start the process – but then understandably question why on earth they are sharing their full home address with a faceless vacuum cleaner company. These factors often mean that a person never ends up benefiting from the guarantee that may have swayed them into purchasing the product in the first place. If a guarantee comes with a product, it's nearly always worth validating it by registration as soon as possible.

What is a warranty? A warranty is a bit like taking out insurance on an item. It is usually something you pay for in addition to the item (although sometimes 'free warranties' are offered as an incentive to buy a certain product, much like guarantees). Many of us will be tempted to get a warranty on our pricier purchases – they usually offer greater protection than a guarantee (for example, may cover accidental damage) and typically last much longer. Warranties are usually awkwardly priced at being expensive enough for us to consider whether they are needed, but cheap enough for us to know we will kick ourselves if a problem arises and we haven't purchased one. They are usually suggested at checkout if you are shopping online.

✓ Guarantees and warranties run *alongside* the rights you already have by law. Therefore, if it's still less than 6 months since you made the purchase, utilising the rights we discussed in our pin-stripe shirt example is often easier. If it's after 6 months, though, guarantees and warranties can be really useful. Frankly, if you're prone to breaking things, a warranty can be a great safety net.

✓Believe me, I have made some disastrous purchases in my time, outrageous I tell you – and I have had to pray that the shop has a returns policy. Experience teaches me that you'll usually find information about any returns policy on the receipt, signs by the till, online, or by making a frantic call to customer services.

Purchasing something online

If you buy an item online, out of a magazine or over the phone, you can cancel the order from the very moment it is placed, right up until 14 days after you have received it. Once you have notified the seller that you wish to cancel the order, you then have 14 days to return the goods.

If something you ordered does not arrive

I have childhood memories of watching the live delivery tracker when I had new gadgets being delivered. I still do it sometimes, refreshing the page over the course of the day. In that nervous observation of the moving blue dot, or the text's promise 'On its way', is the implicit fear: what if it never arrives?

The general rule is that it's the responsibility of the person sending the goods to make sure that you receive them.

A few pointers, though …

- Royal Mail deliver most items in the UK. If Royal Mail deliver to your neighbour because you aren't in (which they often do), it's not the seller's or Royal Mail's fault if you cannot retrieve the item from your neighbour or it is never found after having been left with them.

- If your item was delivered by courier and they left it in the location specified, it is not the seller's responsibility if the item has gone missing.
- If the item was delivered to a location other than that which you agreed, then the seller is required to sort out the issue. If you still want your item, you can ask for a redelivery.

You might, however, think, '… hmm … I'd rather have a refund.' You can ask for one if you don't get the item either:

- within 30 days of buying it;
- on the date you agreed with the seller – but only if you made it clear to the seller when ordering that it was essential to receive it by then (for example for an event, like a graduation gown); or
- on the date of the second-chance delivery you agreed with the seller.

✓ Do you have a sneaky suspicion that your neighbour is keeping hold of your deliveries without telling you? Maybe their fashion sense is starting to look a little too similar to yours … If this sounds like your situation, you might want to opt out of deliveries being given to your neighbour in the future. The Royal Mail have a form on their website enabling you to do this. Items that cannot be delivered will be returned to your local Royal Mail Delivery Office for you to collect, or you can arrange a redelivery. If buying products online where Royal Mail are not the courier, always look out for the 'write a delivery note' textbox. Here you can add any preferences.

Misleading special offers

Remember that time last year when you raced to buy a product on 'limited offer for 1 more day!' … and that same product is still on limited offer now? So do I. This can be particularly frustrating as the money you hastily parted ways with could have been used on something else had you known you had more time.

Misleading special offers should not be made. If the misleading action was a 'significant factor' in encouraging you to buy the product, you may have rights to do something about it.

Purchasing a sofa (an example)

You've purchased a sofa and one of the following scenarios apply:

- You were falsely told that the sofa was only available for a very limited period of time, meaning you felt you had to make an immediate decision and subsequently didn't get sufficient time to make an informed choice.
- The sofa was advertised as 'on offer', but has actually been 'on offer' longer than it was at full price.

Three things you may wish to do are as follows:

1. Gather evidence. This can sometimes be difficult, but if, for example, you can take date-marked screenshots from the sofa company's website, demonstrating that the sofa has been 'on offer' longer than it was at full price, this can be helpful. Also keep receipts.

2. Once you have your evidence, inform the retailer of your concerns and send them your evidence with a letter. You will need to demonstrate to them that this was a significant factor in encouraging you to buy the product. Writing this letter may be enough to encourage the shop to sort things out for you (i.e. accept a return of the sofa and provide you with a refund, even if it isn't faulty). (It is worth viewing the websites of the organisations listed at the back of the book that deal with consumer rights related issues for additional information on this step, including how you may be able to exercise your rights.)

3. If this doesn't solve the problem, you could contact your local trading standards department (for example, google '[Manchester] trading standards'). You will normally be presented with a link to the trading standards part of your city council's website. Trading standards investigate unfair trading and can take businesses to court. While they are not able to get you a refund, the fact that they can take businesses to court can help take problematic companies off the streets.

✓ If you take a photo on a smartphone, you can usually click on the photo's properties and see the time and date that the photo was taken. Similarly, if you take a screenshot on your laptop, you can do the same thing. This can help strengthen your evidence.

Charged the wrong amount of money

In the digitalised world we live in it happens less, but sometimes the price displayed on the price tag may be different to the price we are met with at the till. We've all been there. You might even realise only once you have left the shop and are on your way home. Are they in the wrong? Are you? Will police be waiting at your door when you get home ready to whisk you away for an honest mistake? Who will look after the cat if they do?

Laptops and coffee (examples)

Three scenarios:

- Let's say you have found an item on the shelf labelled at £50. When you get to the till they say, 'Oops – we missed off a zero – it's actually £500' (which, admittedly, is reasonable as it *is* a laptop). If you have not yet purchased the item, you have no legal right to buy the product at the lower price. Of course, you can always ask, but you have no legal rights.

- Let's say you take the laptop to the till, the shop assistant scans it, you buy it, and when you get home you realise you have only been charged £50 when you should have been charged £500. There is no legal requirement for you to give the laptop back. The only way in which the retailer could legally ask you for more money is if you'd *discussed* the price – e.g. 'Wow, £500 is a great price for this laptop!' – but then they inadvertently charged you £50. This is because you will have communicated the price you thought you were paying, and the lesser sum actually charged was clearly known to both you and the seller to be a mistake. Where you haven't discussed the price before paying, it would be difficult for a seller to evidence that you knew the correct price.

- Let's say you grab a coffee, look at your receipt, and think, 'why did my cup of coffee just cost me £25?' Quite simply, go back to the shop and ask to be refunded the difference. You are perfectly within your rights to do this, whether you've been overcharged for a coffee, or a jacket. Common mistakes like this, where the evidence is clear, should be easily rectifiable.

Unhappy with a service

Your partner is about to move into your flat with you, so you pay a professional cleaner to get it in tip-top condition before they do. You arrive back home to see that, while somebody has clearly applied a bit of spray to a few of the windows, the cleaning is at a standard far below what you deem to be acceptable. Let me give you some examples of how the law operates when services are not up to scratch. The key piece of legislation here is the Consumer Rights Act 2015, which sets out your entitlements from contracts involving the supply of services – e.g. a hairdresser, dry cleaner or car mechanic – in addition to the sale of goods discussed previously.

Key things to know

The four key things you need to know are that a service must be carried out:

1. with reasonable care and skill;
2. within a reasonable time;
3. for a reasonable price; and
4. that information about the trader or service is legally binding.

Reasonable care and skill

The services must be carried out to the same or a similar standard to that which is considered acceptable within the trade or profession. A good way to get a benchmark of this is to look at any relevant 'Codes of Practice' for that industry. From this you can assess to what extent you feel the service you received accorded with this Code of Practice, and then whether you believe reasonable care and skill was used.

✓ You may wonder how you can find the Codes of Practice. Google is very helpful in this regard. If you type in 'codes of practice [insert service here]', you will normally be directed to a helpful link. For example, if you type in 'codes of practice garage repairs' you will be directed to the 'Service and Repair Code – The Motor

Ombudsman', which is exactly what you were looking for – you just didn't know it yet.

Within a reasonable time

Often the time at which the task is to be completed will be clearly known to you – e.g. next-day dry cleaners. If they fail to meet this, or a time was not set in the first place and they fail to complete it 'within a reasonable time', the service provider is likely to have breached this obligation. The webpage displaying the Codes of Practice for the service (as referred to above) can often give an indication of what may be deemed a reasonable time; it will always depend on the type of service being provided.

Reasonable price

The price may be agreed in advance of you using the service. In fact, for many services, this will be a legal requirement. If it is not, the price you are charged must be reasonable. This is 'fact-specific', but for a good benchmark see if other people in the area are providing a same or similar service charge.

Information about the trader or service is legally binding

This is quite simple. If the hairdresser says 'we only use natural, organic, non-animal-tested hair products on our clients', and on this basis you use their service, it is important that they do, actually, use the said type of hair products.

✓ Your local dry cleaner may have a sign in the window saying 'we take no responsibility for any loss or damage'. It is important to know that this does not enable them to completely opt out of their responsibilities! By the very virtue of them being dry cleaners, they still must act with 'reasonable care and skill'. If a dry cleaner acting with 'reasonable care and skill' would not have damaged your item, you may be entitled to a remedy.

Remedies

If the service doesn't appear to have been carried out in a manner that accords with the above, the trader may have breached their contract with you. This would mean you would be entitled to something called a 'legal remedy'.

There are two main legal remedies in these circumstances:

- 'Right to repeat performance': in other words, they do the service again.
- 'Right to a price reduction': if the service is something that can't be done again, you are entitled to a price reduction. By way of a general example of how a price reduction might apply, if the service to be provided related to the full cleaning of your car, but only the outside was properly cleaned, it might be the case that you pay an amount that is reflective of what was actually done, as opposed to what should have been done.

Being refused a service

Imagine going to a restaurant and being refused service because of the colour of your skin, or because you were holding hands with your partner. What's the law?

The legal obligations for providers of services are set out in Chapter 2, Part 3 of the Equality Act 2010. If a service provider refuses to provide you a service, or perhaps charges you more, or disadvantages you in any other way, it may be discrimination if it is based on a 'protected characteristic'. These are as follows:

- age – if you're 18 or over (exceptions apply)
- disability
- gender reassignment
- pregnancy and maternity (exceptions apply)
- race
- religion or belief (exceptions apply)
- sex
- sexual orientation (exceptions apply)

(Note: marriage and civil partnership are also protected characteristics, but they only apply in the workplace.)

A 'service provider' is a person concerned with the provision of a service to the public. It can be a business, an individual or a public body. Even if they provide their service for free, they must still comply with the law. (There are some exceptions, as highlighted above.)

If you feel you have been discriminated against, you may want to make a complaint to the service provider first. See p. 260 for advice on how to write a complaint letter.

If you wish to take legal action, you have 6 months less 1 day from when the act of discrimination took place to do so.

4

Transport

If you need to travel between London and Liverpool – check flights first. You may find that flying via Barcelona is cheaper than catching a direct train.

In all seriousness though, it can cost a pretty penny to travel around the UK. This chapter is going to touch on the many ways you can do it, from train, to taxi, to owning your own car.

In terms of train travel, rest assured – I will do my upmost to resist the urge to rant about the privatisation of our rail system, regional wealth disparity, and the contrast between the shiny and slick trains in London and the South East and the trains in parts of the North of England that look like dilapidated caravans. Instead, I will keep it simple and inform you of the key things you need to know so that, when imperfect things happen on our imperfect train system, you can receive the compensation you are entitled to.

In a pursuit to avoid having somebody's armpit in their

face during their commute to work, some people invest in a
car. 'Even if it costs me a bit more in the long run, it's much
more comfortable!' they reason to themselves. People often
don't realise how expensive a car is to run until they have
one for themselves. Friends also have the habit of thinking cars are fuelled on friendship and good conversation as
opposed to petrol that you have to pay for when chauffeur-
ing them around. If the expected costs of cars are bad, the
ones you don't expect are even worse, from problems with
the gearbox, to parking fines. Sometimes you will deserve
a parking fine, but other times, you might want to consider
appealing. Perhaps the sign that had the typically algebraic
message, 'No parking Monday to Friday 9–6 except for permit
holders, on bank holidays only – if it is a leap year' was actually obstructed by an overgrown tree and, as such, you didn't
see it. This chapter will tell you how you can appeal your
ticket in those situations.

Taxis are frequently the night-out transport mode of
choice. We've all had a nightmare in a taxi – being sat in the
cab in silent horror watching the numbers on the meter rise;
or worse still – an amount is demanded by the driver that
bears absolutely no correlation to the short distance travelled.

We spend so much of our lives travelling somewhere that
we ought to know our rights while in the process.

Trains

'We are sorry to announce that the, 0725 service to, Manchester Oxford Road, is delayed by approximately, 104 minutes.' It would be funny if this weren't a genuine announcement that those living in Manchester's surrounding areas are all too familiar with. But the good news is that if your train does get you to your destination late, you may be entitled to compensation.

'Delay Repay'

Most UK train companies are part of a scheme called 'Delay Repay'. When travelling with a train company offering Delay Repay, you are legally entitled to the following:

- a 50 per cent refund if you arrive at your destination 30 minutes late or more
- a full refund if you arrive at your destination 1 hour late or more
- a full refund if your train is cancelled

Some train companies also offer compensation if your train is delayed by 15 minutes or more. It does not matter why your train was delayed/cancelled. Claims for Delay Repay can be made up to 28 days after your journey.

You are not required to have been booked on the specific train that was delayed to make use of Delay Repay. As long as you were lawfully travelling on it, you will usually be able to claim compensation.

Your train does not need to be going to a different town or city in order to benefit from Delay Repay. You could be travelling from one station in a city to another.

The vast majority of train companies are part of the Delay Repay scheme, but, if the train company you used is not, head over to their website where they should have information on what to do in the case of delays.

If this brings no luck, you may be entitled to compensation through the 'National Rail Conditions of Carriage', but two things to note:

- You won't receive as much compensation as you would under Delay Repay.
- You will only be compensated if the delay was the train company's fault (so, no compensation if the delay is caused by the 'wrong snow' on the railway tracks).

Usually, the quickest way to claim compensation for any delay is to visit the website of the train company where you can get further information. Remember to keep hold of your ticket as proof of travel!

✓ It is a good idea to snap a photo of your train ticket the moment you arrive at your destination late. Many train companies allow you to submit a photo of your ticket as proof of travel. This means that if you lose the physical copy of your ticket, you can still get your compensation.

✓ As a consumer, remember you also have rights under the Consumer Rights Act 2015 that may entitle you to compensation

– for example, if the service was not carried out with reasonable care and skill. See Chapter 3, on shopping, for more information on the Consumer Rights Act.

Accessibility

There is a requirement on all licensed train and station operators to establish and comply with an Accessible Travel Policy (ATP) in order to help disabled and older passengers. While the assistance offered by each operator will vary, at a minimum, all operators must provide:

- **Passenger Assist:** This is a service provided by train companies and needs to be booked in advance. Among other things, the service can assist you in reserving wheel-chair spaces and seats, meet you at the station entrance, assist you in coming on and off trains, and assist with any animals you may be travelling with (e.g. guide dogs). At the time of writing, you can book assistance through Passenger Assist until 10 p.m. the day before travel. Head over to the website of the train company you will be travelling with for more information. (Note: sometimes, life means that it will not always be possible to arrange assistance in advance. In such a situation, passengers *can* turn up to a station and request assistance – this service is known as 'Turn Up and Go' – however, it depends on staff availability and other conditions at the time of travel.)
- **Alternative Accessible Transport:** Operators must ensure that you can make as much of your journey by

rail as possible. They should organise an alternative, accessible service, such as a replacement bus, if for some reason you cannot use a rail service.

- **Tickets and fares:** If you are unable to purchase a ticket at a station before your journey, you will be able to do so without being charged extra while on the train or at the destination.
- **Scooter carriage:** Operators must not only set out their policy on the carrying of mobility scooters and other mobility aids on their trains, but also make the reasoning behind their policy clear.
- **Passenger information:** Up-to-date information must be provided by operators about the accessibility of services and facilities.
- **Aural and visual information:** Operators must provide, wherever possible, aural and visual information on train departures that is clear and consistent.
- **Luggage:** Operators must ensure that staff will be available to assist you with your luggage where this has been arranged in advance.
- **Ramps:** Ramps that are fit for purpose must be available at all staffed stations to help you board or leave the train, regardless of whether or not assistance has been booked in advance. If the assistance is required at an unstaffed station and has been booked in advance, a member of staff with a ramp must be available.

✓ Have you checked if you are eligible for a Disabled Persons Railcard (DPRC)? If you are, you could receive up to a third off on train travel. While on the topic of railcards – it is always worth checking if you are eligible for one as they can offer significant discounts. Google 'national railcards' to check your eligibility. I have a 26–30 Railcard, but you might be entitled to, say, an HM Forces Railcard, or a Senior Railcard if you are aged 60 or over.

Somebody is in my seat

Bylaw 19 of the Railway Bylaws states:

> *Classes of accommodation, reserved seats and sleeping berths*
>
> Except with permission from an authorised person, no person shall remain in any seat, berth or any part of a train where a notice indicates that it is reserved for a specified ticket holder or holders of tickets of a specific class, except the holder of a valid ticket entitling him to be in that particular place.

This means you have every right to ask somebody to budge from your reserved seat.

Taxis

Not all taxis are equal. Hopping in a cab sounds straightforward enough, but depending on the type of vehicle you are in, different rules apply. Clueing yourself up on your taxi rights will not only save you money, but also give you peace of mind. It's always helpful to know how you can respond if something goes wrong.

Different rules apply depending on whether you are in a hackney carriage or a private hire vehicle.

Hackney carriages

You have a job interview in an unfamiliar city. After stepping off the train you follow the signs to 'taxis'. You see a taxi rank and eight taxis, all similar-looking, lined up. These will be hackney carriages.

How to identify them:

- Hackney carriages are the traditional 'black cabs' (although they come in all different colours, depending on what city you're in). They can be hailed on the street and can park in taxi ranks. They usually have a large roof light with 'taxi' written on it.

Your rights in one:

- Their fares are set by the council so if the taxi driver tells you a fare different to that on the meter you can immediately complain to them – it is illegal – or make a note of the fare, ask for a receipt, and contact the council so that it can investigate.

✓ Contrary to popular belief, a hackney carriage driver cannot refuse a journey due to it being too short. You can report this to the local council if it happens.

Private hire vehicles (including Uber)

It's a hot summer day and you are having a picnic with friends at the park. As the evening draws in, you start making plans to get home. Your friend opens an app on his phone and mutters something about it always being him who has to pay for the ride. You jump in.

An Uber, or any minicab, is an example of a private hire vehicle.

How to identify them:

- They often have door signs saying 'advance bookings only'.
- They often look like the 'normal' type of car your mum or dad would drive.
- They cannot be hailed on the street and must be booked in advance, usually over the phone or via an app.

Your rights in one:

- Their fares are not set by the council so clarify in advance what the fare will be. If you are overcharged, tell the driver of the agreed fare. If this doesn't work, call the phone operator to explain (for private hire services that are solely app-based, there will normally be a complaints section within the app).
- Complaints can only be made through the private hire company itself but this is still worth doing because they won't want to damage their reputation.

✓ Many people unknowingly incur extra charges on their fares. Just using the boot of a hackney carriage can add an extra 20p to your fare in some council areas. Private hire vehicles also apply extra charges, so it is always something worth checking.

Driving

Running a car is like running a small household. There are always costs that you could not have envisaged. You will have just got on top of your finances and your exhaust pipe will fall off for no apparent reason. You often don't realise parts of the car exist until you need to pay for them to be fixed. If fixing a car didn't cost enough, try parking it. Driving a car comes with significant responsibility too. After all, you are in control of a 1.5-tonne object that can, if driven poorly, cause serious damage. This section will walk you through some of the information all drivers ought to know.

Parking tickets

If you illegally park on the road or in a local authority car park ...

You are rushing to a job interview and think, 'Let me just park on the double yellow lines, or in this local authority car park without paying.' When you return to your car you find a bright-yellow sticker on your windshield (or perhaps receive a letter through the door some days later). How do they work?

- You can receive a Penalty Charge Notice (PCN) – loosely defined as a 'fine'.

- The amount you are charged is laid down by law, so you can't negotiate. You will usually have 28 days to pay, but the fine is reduced if you pay within 14 days, so it's often worth just biting the bullet, facing the shame and paying up promptly.

- You can appeal if you feel some form of error has been made. Perhaps your car wasn't technically on the double yellow lines, or you did actually pay. In any event, it's important to have evidence. See p. 108 for ideas of the types of things that can serve as good evidence.

If you park in a private car park …

It's 8.57 a.m. Your barber opens his shop at 9 a.m. You don't want anybody else to get in the barber chair before you as you have a busy day ahead – and each extra customer is an extra 30 minutes in the waiting area. In the corner of your eye you spot an old courtyard that a private car parking operator has transformed into parking spaces, available to members of the public at a cost. You park your car, lock it, and off you sprint to the barber shop. When you return to your car, you find a bright-yellow sticker on your windshield (or perhaps receive a letter through the door some days later). You cast your mind back, trying to figure out if you forgot to pay, or alternatively if an error has been made. You turn to this book to remind yourself of the law.

- If you receive a ticket when parking in a private car park, confusingly, this is also called a PCN, but stands for *Parking Charge Notice*.
- The notice put on your car is simply an invoice. It is effectively saying, 'Hey – we believe you've breached a contract with us by not paying when you parked in our car park. As explained on our signs, not paying may result in us seeking a payment from you – this is us seeking that payment.'
- Private car parking operators *cannot* clamp your car (save for in some very limited circumstances).
- Private car parking operators are able to contact the Driver and Vehicle Licensing Agency (DVLA) in order to get your address if they want to send your notice in the post. This might be the case if the car park is monitored using cameras that capture the arrival/exit times of all vehicles and is able to identify those that have failed to pay or have overstayed.
- If you don't pay, a private company needs to go to court to get money off you.

✓ Private car parking operators have to comply with a Code of Practice. The Code of Practice will be managed by one of two trade associations – either the British Parking Association (BPA) or the International Parking Community (IPC). Trade associations publish their Code on their website and have processes to assist motorists if they believe the Code may have been breached. It is anticipated that the government will soon introduce one single Code of Practice.

✓For any appeal process, evidence is key. If your argument is that a sign you were supposed to have read was not visible, go back to the location and take a picture of it that demonstrates how difficult it is to see. If the ticket you purchased had fallen off your dashboard and thus wasn't seen by the inspector, provided you still have it, take a photo of the ticket as proof of purchase. Be creative and 'hands on' with your evidence – what can you prove about the day in question to persuade the company, or a court? Do you have a text to a friend saying 'just paying for my parking – will be with you in 5 mins'? If the company believe that your evidence would be strong enough to persuade a court, this may dissuade them from taking any further action against you.

✓An ethical point: of course, if you are in the wrong, just pay. It is worth knowing that paying a parking ticket is often deemed as you admitting that it was rightly given to you – making it harder to appeal later downstream.

Faults with your vehicle

If the police identify a fault with your vehicle, such as a broken brake light, they may give you a 'vehicle defect rectification notice'.

This will require that you get your vehicle fixed, and you will have 14 days from the date of the notice to provide proof to the police that this has been done. Depending on the type of fault, a receipt from your mechanic could be sufficient proof.

You can also receive a fine and points on your licence for defects with your vehicle – for example, using a vehicle with defective steering, defective tyres or defective brakes can result in 3 penalty points.

Speeding

Speeding can kill. This book in no way seeks to encourage bad driving. There are occasions, however, where despite being the good careful driver you are, you perhaps don't realise that a speed limit has changed, or maybe don't realise the needle on the speedometer has crept a few mph over what it should be.

If you are caught speeding, a Notice of Intended Prosecution (NIP) will be issued: if by a speed camera, this will be posted to the registered keeper of the vehicle; or if by a police officer, this may be given verbally to the driver.

In post form, the NIP is a formal letter with the words 'Notice of Intended Prosecution' printed on it. You are required to fill in the NIP and then send it back in the post. On it you can tick that, for example, you were not the driver of the vehicle, and will have the space to write the actual driver's name and address. The person whom you name as the driver will then receive a NIP addressed to them. Alternatively, if it was you driving, you can confirm that you were the driver. If you do this, you will receive a further letter detailing your options. This may include the option(s) of:

- accepting a conditional offer of a Fixed Penalty Notice (the minimum that can be issued for speeding is £100 and comes with 3 penalty points); and/or
- going on a speed awareness course. Attending a speed awareness course will result in you not receiving points

on your licence or a fine (but the course itself costs money – roughly £100).

You can also tick an option saying that you wish to go to court. You might tick this if, for example, you accept you were the driver of the vehicle but believe your speed was recorded inaccurately, or so that any mitigating circumstances you may have can be considered.

You will not get a conviction if you pay the fixed penalty or attend the speed awareness course. If you don't respond to the NIP, the matter will go to the magistrates' court. Failure to provide the information required for the NIP can result in a £1,000 fine, 6 points on your licence, and potentially disqualification in the event that you are likely to accumulate 12 or more points on your licence. Similarly, if you are a new driver (in your two-year probationary period), the imposition of 6 or more points within this period may result in your licence being revoked by the DVLA.

It is also worth knowing that if the offence is particularly serious – for example you are considerably over the speed limit – the matter may go straight to court without you receiving a NIP.

Driving without insurance

Your flatmate asks you to pop to the shop to get some milk, but it's chucking it down with rain. Your car insurance expired a couple of days ago, and you haven't got round to sorting it out. 'The shop is only around the corner,' you think, and you hop into your uninsured car. You are then stopped by the police who learn you are driving without insurance. What happens?

Well, the fact of the matter is that you are driving and have no insurance – so the offence is made out. This means it doesn't hold weight to say, for example, 'I didn't know I wasn't insured.' You will still be deemed guilty of the offence and receive a conviction or be offered a conditional offer of a fixed penalty of 6 points and a £300 fine. If convicted, it is very possible that points will be put on your driving licence and you could even be disqualified if you have pre-existing points, and, with the new points, your total is 12 or more. It is possible to make arguments to the court that may persuade it not to put points on your licence or disqualify you. Such an argument might be that you genuinely didn't know you were uninsured or that you were driving due to an emergency.

✓ If you are found to be driving without insurance in the course of your employment and were not aware that there was not any insurance allowing you to drive, this is a completely different story. If the court accepts what you are saying to be true, you will have a defence to the charge and subsequently will not be convicted. Your employer could still get in trouble, though.

✓ There is an offence called 'causing death while driving unlicensed, disqualified or uninsured'. This offence carries a maximum sentence of 2 years. To be found guilty of this offence, there does not need to be *any* evidence that you were to blame for the death. If we take the example earlier about hopping into the car to get some milk for your flatmate, let's say while you are driving a jogger with his headphones on runs into the road and into the path of the car, tragically causing a fatal collision. Even if your driving was brilliant and you made every effort to avoid him, you could still be found guilty of this offence as you should not have been on the road without a driving licence, while disqualified or while uninsured in the first place.

Using your phone and satnav

Holding a phone or satnav while driving is illegal. Use of hands-free equipment, however, is not illegal, so you can use a dashboard holder or windscreen mount to hold your device in place, and you can also use your car's built-in satnav. Bluetooth headsets and using voice command technology such as Apple's 'Siri' are legal too – but still, don't let them be a distraction.

Holding your phone while driving can result in 6 penalty points and a £200 fine. The punishment could be more severe if it is dealt with by a court. Getting 6 or more points within 2 years of passing your test will lead to you losing your driving licence. You will be required to retake both parts of your test.

✓ An offence you should also know about is that of not being in proper control of your vehicle. Putting your make-up on or eating a packet of crisps while driving are examples of things that might amount to this. You could get 3 penalty points on your licence and a £100 fine. If the matter goes to court, the punishment could be more severe.

✓ Even if you are stuck in a queue, or at a red light – holding your phone, maybe even just to check your notifications, is illegal.

✓ If you don't have a full view of the road and the traffic, you can get 3 penalty points. Therefore, make sure that in your attempt to be hands-free, you don't buy equipment for your windscreen that stops you properly seeing out of it.

Points on your licence and 'totting up'

If you accrue 12 or more points on your licence within a 3-year period, this will result in you being banned (disqualified) from driving for a minimum of 6 months. This is known as a 'totting up' ban. This is because you have 'totted up' (or accrued) the requisite number of points on your licence to receive an automatic ban.

If you get a second disqualification within 3 years, your ban can last for 12 months. If you get a third disqualification within 3 years, your ban can last for 2 years.

There may be arguments you can make in an effort to persuade a court not to disqualify you if you find yourself in the position of having 12 points – for example, that the ban would cause you or others exceptional hardship. Exceptional hardship is an argument that will need to be made in court and can only be used as an argument to avoid a ban once in a 3-year period. Having supporting evidence will often be important and you may wish to consider speaking to a lawyer (and/or having one represent you in court).

Being disqualified for 56 days or more will mean you'll need to apply for a new driving licence (note: not retake your test, just apply for a new licence. Nonetheless, in some situations the court *will* state that you will need to retake your driving test, or take something called an extended driving test – which is more difficult than the standard type of driving test. This extended driving test is often ordered if someone is convicted of a more serious offence, such as dangerous driving). If you are disqualified for less than 56 days, you won't need to apply for a new licence. Just be sure you don't drive until the 56 days have ended. To be extra safe, it is worth checking with the court and/or the DVLA before you do.

✓You can check when your disqualification ends by going to gov.uk/view-driving-licence.

✓Head to p. 255 for more information on when the police can pull you over while driving, and to p. 205 for information on drinking and driving.

5

Healthcare

Much of this book was written during the Covid-19 pandemic, the biggest health crisis in living memory. I, probably like you, know people that have suffered serious illness as a result of the virus, or sadly passed away. It has been a reminder that our bodies are not invincible. Even in ordinary times, sometimes a spell of bad health is unavoidable. It is a humbling experience when your wellbeing lies in the hands of the doctors and nurses treating you. Our National Health Service (NHS) is brilliant but it is also imperfect. Through many years of austerity, the NHS has been heavily under-funded, under-resourced and remains layered in numerous levels of bureaucracy. Crucially, it comprises ordinary human beings who, no matter how well trained, are capable – just like you and I – of making errors of judgement or getting things wrong. There is nothing more important than your health and therefore you, more than anybody, should look after it. When in the care of medical professionals, there are most certainly points where you will need to delegate full responsibility to them and trust that they will do their best for you. Nonetheless, right up until that point, you need to know as much as you can about what is going on – it's your body, your health, your life.

Within this chapter will be considerable discussion of mental health. Research from the charity Mind shows that, each year, 1 in 4 people in England experience some kind of mental health problem. The 2014 Survey of Mental Health and Wellbeing in England reported that 1 in 6 people aged 16 or over met the criteria for a common mental health disorder such as anxiety or depression. The often invisible nature of mental health makes it a topic frequently omitted in discussions of health. But whether what you're dealing with is visible to others or not, we still retain important legal rights and are absolutely entitled to be treated with care and respect.

This chapter will inform you of some of the essentials when it comes to your healthcare – from who can see your medical records, to when you can see your child's medical records, to what happens if you are detained under the Mental Health Act.

Medical records

Your medical records are where notes are kept about your health and the care you've received from medical providers in the past. They're kept so that you can be given the best continuity of care and for medicolegal purposes. They might include notes on your allergies, any illnesses you've had, medication you've been prescribed and any results of tests or X-rays. They may also include information on your lifestyle, like whether you smoke or drink. In other words, it's fairly personal information – and nobody wants to feel their medical records are not private. As such, safeguards need to be in place to protect this information. This section will explore the principles at play, when it is possible for other people to see your records and when you can see theirs.

Your right to view your medical records

You have the legal right to see your medical records. You do not need to provide an explanation as to why you want to see them. Many GP surgeries now allow you to view your GP records online, but you will have to register to use this service. Speak to your GP surgery about this.

You can make a formal request to see your medical records (and in fact, any records an organisation holds about you) under the General Data Protection Regulation (GDPR). This is called making a 'subject access request'. More information on how to do this can be found on p. 263.

Access to your medical records can be limited or denied by health professionals. This could be because, for example, the clinician believes that you seeing your medical records might be harmful to your mental or physical health.

If you are dissatisfied with the outcome of a subject access request, you should first complain to the organisation, but then can make a complaint to the Information Commissioner's Office (ICO). For further information, contact the ICO or view their resources online (see p. 280).

Who else can view your medical records?

Other healthcare teams involved in your care

Due to your medical records being confidential, nobody else should be shown them without your consent. Sensible, right?

It won't surprise you, though, to find out that information may be shared with other NHS or social care staff involved in your care. This in principle should make things that bit easier for you. They do this under an 'implied consent'. In other words, although you haven't expressly written or said the words 'you can share my medical records', it is reasonable to think that you would consent to the information being shared. If you explicitly inform an NHS service that your records should not be passed to another party, they cannot do so under implied consent. Nonetheless, there are occasions when the sharing of the information may still be deemed necessary – such as if you lack capacity and it is deemed that sharing the information is in your best interests (we will be discussing capacity in greater detail later), or if it is in the public interest that your records be shared (perhaps to protect others).

Other people

In answer to the question of whether other individuals – like your football friend Jerome – can view your records, the basic answer is a resounding NO. He would only be able to do so if he was acting on your behalf with your consent, had the legal authority to make decisions on your behalf (power of attorney), or had some other legal basis of access.

He could also make a subject access request for this information, but would need your written consent. This is true of all other adults – including your parents or partner.

Viewing other people's medical records

Your children

You may think that access to your child's medical records would be automatic, but children also have the right to privacy. If you are a parent, whether or not you can access your children's medical records somewhat depends on their age. As per the NHS website:

- If your child is 12 or younger, you will usually be able to access their records.
- If your child is 13 or older, the position is a little different. At the age of 13, children will usually be considered as having the capacity to give or refuse consent to their parents' requests to access their health records, and so your child will usually be asked if they are happy for you to have access.

✓British Medical Association guidance states that clinicians should make efforts to encourage children to involve their parents in their medical care.

Accessing the medical records of a loved one who is ill

In the same way that others cannot access your medical records when you are ill, you cannot access the medical records of someone else if they are ill and unable to consent – even if they are your partner or parent. For this, you would need to be a lasting Power of Attorney for Health and Welfare (more on this later).

Accessing the medical records of a loved one who has passed away

When it comes to a person's medical records, these remain confidential – even in death. Only certain people can view the records of someone who has passed away. According to the Access to Health Records Act 1990, you must be either:

- the personal representative of the person who has died (such as the executor or administrator of the person's estate), or
- someone who may have a claim resulting from the person's death.

✓The Access to Health Records Act 1990 gives a right of access to information directly relevant to a claim, *not* the full medical record.

Treatment

Consent

The law is very clear on the fact that, as the owner of *your* body, it is you who should be able to make decisions on whether or not you receive treatment – even if this could cause you harm. This makes sense, but in case you are not in the position to make such a decision, safeguards are in place too.

Your consent is required before any treatment, examination or intervention (except when authorised under mental health legislation – more on this later). In most cases you have the right to refuse treatment, even if this could result in serious harm or your death.

Some fundamental principles for you to know are as follows:

- If there are different options as to the treatments you can receive, you should be informed about these.
- If a clinician does not think a certain type of treatment is appropriate, you cannot force them to give it to you.
- Consent needs to be obtained from a patient prior to examination. This could be given orally, in writing or could be implied – for example, rolling up your sleeve and offering your arm to the clinician so that your blood pressure can be taken.
- If an examination or treatment is forced on you against your will, the clinician's actions could amount to a

criminal offence. You may wish to make a complaint to the relevant NHS trust or Clinical Commissioning Group (CCG), or the police.

Capacity and refusal

For your consent to be valid you first and foremost must have the capacity to make the decision. If you are aged 16 or over you are presumed to have the capacity to consent to treatment unless there is evidence to the contrary. To have capacity to consent means that you understand the information being given to you and can use it to make an informed decision which you are able to communicate. The Mental Capacity Act 2005 says a person is unable to make a decision if they cannot: understand the information relevant to the decision, retain that information, or use or weigh up that information as part of the process of making the decision. Each and every case is decided on its own merits, and in the moment of when a decision is being made. Therefore, if your mind is impaired at any given time meaning you are unable to make a decision, you lack capacity in that moment. Being drunk or otherwise intoxicated may mean you lack capacity for certain things for a certain amount of time. A health condition such as dementia or bipolar disorder may also affect your capacity in certain moments. In addition, capacity is not linear – someone considered as not having the capacity to make a decision today may be considered as having the capacity to do so tomorrow.

Capacity is also determined by the decision being made.

You may have the capacity to make certain decisions for yourself (e.g. agree to an examination of your mouth due to a pain from your wisdom tooth), but lack the capacity to make other decisions (e.g. what cancer treatment you should receive).

The consent must also be voluntary and informed. 'Voluntary' means that the decision to consent is *yours*. It has not been brought about through, for example, pressure from clinicians or members of your family. Being 'informed' means that you have been briefed in full about what the treatment involves, including the benefits and risks, any alternatives available, and what will happen if the treatment does not go ahead. You should also be aware that you can refuse treatment.

Your child's treatment

As part of the deep care you have for your child, you may want to get involved with their professional care too – being present at doctor's appointments, researching treatment options online, or even just getting them a cup of tea in the hospital. While these actions are all signs of a loving and caring parent, the following points seek to make you aware of where a line can legally be drawn.

- A clinician is able to provide a child with treatment they believe to be necessary, even if the parent or guardian (I will simply say 'parent' moving forward) does not give consent for the child to be treated.

- A clinician can do whatever is necessary to save a child's life if it is in danger.
- If the parent unreasonably refuses medical treatment or medical attention for the child or fails to seek it altogether, they could be open to prosecution.
- If the child is under 16, they will be able to give consent if they are 'believed to have enough intelligence, competence and understanding to fully appreciate what's involved in their treatment' (NHS website).
- If the child is under 16, has sufficient understanding and *refuses* treatment, then clinicians can still carry out the treatment if it is deemed to be in the child's best interests with the parent's consent or by a court order.
- A person aged 16 or 17 can give consent to their own treatment independently of their parent. If they cannot give their consent – perhaps due to serious disability, or incapacity – the consent of the parent must be obtained.
- A person aged 16 or 17 who has capacity can refuse treatment, but, if treatment is deemed by clinicians to be in their best interests, their refusal can be overridden by the consent of either a parent or the courts.

✓Google 'fraser guidelines' for information on the principles used specifically to decide if a child can consent to contraceptive or sexual health advice and treatment.

Making an 'advance decision' (living will)

Many can find reading about capacity daunting. They worry that what they may truly have wanted may not be done by those looking after their care if they ever reach a point where they lack capacity. It is therefore important to know that if you are aged 18 or over, you can make what is known as an 'advance decision'. This is basically where you can state any medical treatments that you refuse to have if there is a time in the future where you do not have the capacity to make such a decision. It will often be a good idea to make your advance decision with your clinician's support. Your advance decision needs to be written by you, signed and dated by you in the presence of a witness, and signed and dated by your witness. The NHS website contains more information – all of which is important to follow to ensure that your advance decision is completed correctly. Your advance decision will be legally binding as long as it is valid and applicable.

Lasting Power of Attorney

A lasting Power of Attorney is a legal document. It is created by you while you have the mental capacity to do so. In the document, you grant another person the power to manage your affairs should you not have the mental capacity to do so yourself. It might sound morbid, but actually it's a really sensible way to not only give yourself some peace of mind, but also to look out for the future version of you. Many of us assume that if we become ill our parent(s) or partner will be able to look after us and deal with our medical affairs without issue. The reality is that without the creation of a lasting Power of Attorney authorising this, these people will come to the unfortunate realisation that they cannot make decisions for us.

There are two types of power of attorney: 'lasting Power of Attorney – Property and Financial Affairs' and 'lasting Power of Attorney – Health and Welfare'. With this being the medical chapter, we are here referring to the latter. This gives authority for another person of your choosing to help you make decisions about your health and welfare.

You have a number of options for creating a lasting Power of Attorney. You can search 'public guardian power of attorney online form' which will direct you to a gov.uk site where you can create a lasting Power of Attorney online. There are clear instructions to assist you. You can also go to a high-street stationer and buy a DIY Power of Attorney kit. Again, the kit will contain instructions on how to create your document. Every day numerous members of the public create a lasting Power of Attorney without any external support; however, many solicitors offer the drawing up of a Power of Attorney as a service – this is something you can certainly take up if you feel it will afford you peace of mind.

✓ You can appoint more than one attorney whom you can instruct to make decisions either 'jointly' (meaning that your attorneys must make decisions together and unanimously) or 'jointly and severally' (meaning that your attorneys can either act together, or make decisions on their own).

Mental health

In recent years there has been a push for parity in terms of how physical health and mental health are treated. This is important. Mental health conditions often carried a stigma in the past, and there is a long history of poor treatment and misunderstanding. Today, things are better (though of course there's always more to do), and we can use the NHS for mental health treatment that includes medication and talking therapies.

When your mental health is in crisis, there are a few options for seeking help. You may go to your GP, you may be referred to a community mental health team, or you might talk to a cognitive behavioural therapist, a psychologist or a psychiatrist. In some more extreme cases, it might be that you are sectioned under the Mental Health Act.

This chapter will not suggest care options, but it will cover your rights when it comes to seeking and receiving care.

As with anything concerning the NHS, years of austerity, cuts and underfunding have had an impact on how certain things play out in reality, but what follows is a description of best practice, what you are legally entitled to and what the law says should happen.

The mental health system has three areas: primary, secondary and tertiary care (note: for Child and Adolescent Mental Health Services (CAMHS), a 4-tier system is used. Google 'CAMHS tier system' for more information).

Primary care: This is typically the first point of contact for people in need of healthcare. If you have mild to moderate mental health problems, you will be able to get support and treatment. Primary care services include your GP, your local link worker through your GP and talking therapy.

Secondary care: Secondary care covers general community and hospital care. It is the level up from primary care. Community mental health teams assist people living in the 'community', i.e. outside of hospital, with their mental health care. Generally, you will need a referral from your GP to access secondary services.

Tertiary care: Tertiary care is highly specialist care, covering specialist community and hospital care. It includes, for example, secure forensic mental health services.

Key things to know about being sectioned

The most important piece of legislation to know about when it comes to mental health is the Mental Health Act 1983, which was updated in 2007. If you are likely to have any interactions with mental health services, primary, secondary or tertiary, I would encourage you to read the Mental Health Act 1983 Code of Practice. It's a little dense, but very clearly laid out, and it will give you an insight into how professionals should be carrying out their responsibilities under the Mental Health Act. This will help you make sure that everything is being done correctly.

Here, we will look at one area covered by the Act: being sectioned. This is an instance where your right to liberty (Article 5 of the European Convention on Human Rights – see the Preface on human rights) is limited in a way that isn't the case with other medical treatment, and so it's even more important to understand.

Being sectioned means that you are detained in hospital under one of the 'sections' in this Act. It comes under secondary care. You can be sectioned against your will, and under some sections, can be given treatment without your consent. You can be sectioned for your own health or safety or to protect others. This is, of course, very serious, and as such the law contains strict rules so that sectioning is only done when necessary.

The different sections have different requirements. Therefore, what will happen to you will depend upon which section you are sectioned under. Here we will focus on the ones used most often – Section 2, Section 3, Section 4 and Section 5.

While this part of the book, like most of it, is written on the premise that the person wishing to utilise their rights is the reader, it is acknowledged that depending on the specific circumstances, a person who has been sectioned may not be in a position to read and retain all of this information. With that in mind, this is a part of the book that the friends and family members of those sectioned may wish to familiarise themselves with so that they can best support their loved one.

Mental health assessments

Before you can be sectioned, you must be assessed by health-care professionals to ensure it is necessary. This will usually be at your home or at a hospital.

The team assessing you will normally consist of the following:

- an approved mental health professional (AMHP)
- a registered medical practitioner (such as your GP)
- a Section 12-approved doctor (normally a psychiatrist)

The AMHP should explain to you who the team are, and why you are being assessed. You are well within your rights to ask to see their ID – something they should all have on them.

The AMHP will interview you in order to see if being in hospital is necessary in all of the circumstances to provide you with the care and treatment you need. Both doctors would need to agree with this. The doctors may also ask to assess both your physical and mental state.

You do have rights while you are being assessed. Here are some things to remember:

- **There is no need to do it alone:** You can have somebody with you during the assessment. This might be a friend or family member.
- **Make yourself comfortable:** If you find having the two doctors along with the AMHP daunting, you can ask to speak to the AMHP alone. Nonetheless, they do have the

right to have another professional present – so this may not be possible.

- **You do not have to respond:** Although you will be asked questions, you don't by law have to answer. Remember though: decisions can still be made about you regardless of whether or not you decide to answer questions. Conversely, you may choose to ask questions yourself. The healthcare professionals have a duty to keep you fully informed, and should answer any questions you might have. You can also express your views as to what should happen, but the healthcare professionals do not need to follow these.
- **Language barriers:** It is important that you understand what is being asked of you so you can give the most accurate responses. You have the right to an interpreter. Therefore, if English is not your first language and you would benefit from having an interpreter, inform the AMHP so this can be arranged.

✓ Many people will want to speak to a lawyer before they are sectioned. You are well within your rights to do so. You should be aware that the healthcare professionals are not required to give you time to do this before making their decision on whether you should be sectioned. Your lawyer will also not be able to prevent the sectioning from happening, but they can clue you up on your rights so you know, for example, how to make an application to be discharged from your section.

✓ The AMHP should make arrangements for the immediate care of any individuals you are caring for (such as your children) and any pets if you are going to be taken to hospital. Arrangements should be made to ensure your house is secure if it will be vacant when you are in hospital, too.

✓ Section 135 of the Mental Health Act 1983 enables the police to enter your home without your permission and take you to a place of safety. They require a warrant from the magistrates' court in order to do this and the application for the warrant must be made by an AMHP. The warrant can be issued by the court given that there is reasonable cause to suspect that you have a mental disorder and you:

- have been or are being ill-treated; or
- neglected; or
- are unable to look after yourself.

(I would encourage anybody worrying about Section 135 to read this part of the Act in full so that they can see the precise wording. The above seeks to serve only as an easily understandable summary of the key principles.)

If you are sectioned

It can feel a little abstract to try to remember just the section numbers (e.g. 'Section 2' or 'Section 3'), but each section comes with its own little 'tagline', which can help you remember it, and remind you of your rights under it (I have simplified the tagline applying to Section 5, just to make it easier to remember and understand):

- Section 2 – Admission for Assessment
- Section 3 – Admission for Treatment

- Section 4 – Admission for Assessment in Cases of Emergency
- Section 5 – 'Holding Powers'

It's important to know that under any of these sections, you can only be detained if you have a 'mental disorder'. This assessment will be made by healthcare professionals, as the Mental Health Act does not explicitly state what is classed as a 'mental disorder'.

Section 2 – Admission for Assessment

If you are detained under Section 2, you can be kept in hospital for up to 28 days. This gives doctors the opportunity to assess what, if any, treatment you need.

If you have not been assessed for your mental health in hospital before (or a significant amount of time has elapsed since your last assessment), it is more likely that Section 2 will be used than Section 3.

If you are offered treatment which you refuse, it may be given to you without your consent.

Section 3 – Admission for Treatment

If you are detained under Section 3, you can be kept in hospital for up to 6 months. This can be extended. Section 3 is intended to keep a patient in hospital for treatment.

In order for you to be detained under Section 3, there must be appropriate treatment available for you and your 'nearest relative' has not objected. (Note: the term 'nearest relative' refers to a family member with certain powers and responsibilities if you are detained. It may be different from your next of kin. See Section 26 of the Mental Health Act 1983 for more information.)

You can be given treatment without your consent for 3 months. After 3 months, you can only be given treatment without your consent if a 'second opinion appointed doctor' (an independent doctor appointed by the Care Quality Commission in England or by the Healthcare Inspectorate in Wales) approves it.

Once you leave hospital, you will receive aftercare, known as Section 117 aftercare (as it is covered under Section 117 of the Mental Health Act 1983).

Section 4 – Admission for Assessment in Cases of Emergency

Section 4 is used in emergency situations. Unlike for Section 2 or 3, only one doctor needs to recommend that you are sectioned (along with the AMHP).

You can be kept for up to 72 hours. In this time the hospital will arrange a full assessment and a decision will be made as to whether the Section 4 should be changed to a Section 2.

You can refuse treatment (however, see issues related to capacity discussed earlier).

Section 5 – 'Holding Powers'

Section 5 gives a doctor or nurse the power to prevent you

leaving hospital. If you are a voluntary patient and you want to leave, it is a power that could be used to stop you if it is felt that you are too unwell. Note that Section 5 comprises different subsections. The two discussed in the following paragraphs are Section 5(2) and Section 5(4).

A doctor can hold you under Section 5(2) for up to 72 hours. They should write a report to the hospital managers that details why you need to be detained. During the time of this detention (and as quickly as possible) you should receive an assessment to decide whether you should be detained under Section 2 or 3.

A mental health or learning disability nurse can hold you under Section 5(4) for up to 6 hours. The holding power will end the moment a doctor arrives. You may then be transferred onto a Section 2, 3, or 5(2), or continue as a voluntary patient.

✓ Remember the time periods stated are for how long you *may* be kept in hospital; this refers to the maximum amount of time you are legally allowed to be kept for. The actual time in your situation could be much less.

✓ You do not need to be sectioned in order to get hospital treatment. You can, on a voluntary basis, go into hospital. You may do this if you are becoming concerned about your mental health (for example, if you are feeling suicidal). As a voluntary patient you can technically leave whenever you want and you can also refuse treatment. Section 5 allows the healthcare professionals to stop you leaving though (for example, if they worry that you are too unwell). It is important to know that being a voluntary patient in hospital (as opposed to being sectioned), will mean that you are not entitled to certain things. For example, you do not have the right to Section 117 aftercare, or the right to challenge your detention by applying to a Mental Health Tribunal, or the right to an Independent Mental Health Advocate (IMHA). (Note: this is in England only; in Wales you *do* have the right to an IMHA, even as a voluntary patient. IMHAs will be explained in more detail next.)

Your rights when in hospital

Upon being sectioned and detained in hospital, you should be told why and what will be happening to you, and you should be given information leaflets. If upon your arrival you do not receive these leaflets, you have the right to request them. Direct your request to your IMHA, the ward manager or a senior member of your care staff.

Your IMHA is a person who can support you in understanding your rights under the Mental Health Act. They are there to help you. If you have not been given a copy of your sectioning papers, you can ask your IMHA (or the ward staff), who should be able to help you get them. The Mental Health Act Code of Practice is also worth requesting. It details how those caring for you should be carrying out their responsibilities under the Mental Health Act.

If you are unhappy about your treatment, you can complain to the Care Quality Commission, or if in Wales, the Healthcare Inspectorate.

You have the right to have visitors, some telephone access and also to correspondence with your solicitor. You also have the right to vote.

When you are sectioned, the Mental Health Act gives the power for you to be kept on a locked ward. You can ask your responsible clinician (the mental health care professional who has overall responsibility for your care and treatment) for permission to leave the ward. Section 17 of the Mental Health Act 1983 enables them to do this, but if they allow you to, you may have to abide to certain conditions, such as being back before a certain a time. You may also be able to leave the ward if you are joined by a member of hospital staff. This is known as 'escorted leave'.

You have the right to request and be informed of information regarding your right to apply to a Mental Health Tribunal, as well as how you can contact a mental health solicitor. The Mental Health Tribunal is made up of a judge, a psychiatrist (not one working in the hospital you are in) and a person who has knowledge of mental health care (known as the 'lay member').

Leaving hospital

If you are detained under either Section 2 or 3, you can be discharged by:

- your responsible clinician
- the hospital managers (a panel trained and appointed to review whether people should be discharged. They are

independent of the hospital)
- your 'nearest relative' (note that they can be stopped from discharging you by the responsible clinician)
- the Mental Health Tribunal

You can speak with your IMHA, who will be able to provide more information on these processes. When it comes to making an appeal to the Mental Health Tribunal, it is worth remembering that:

- If you are detained under Section 2 – you can appeal to the tribunal during your first 14 days.
- If you are detained under Section 3 – you can appeal to the tribunal once in the first 6 months and once each time your section is renewed. The renewal is every 12 months and the hearing should take place within 8 weeks of your application.

You have the right to be informed of how you can contact a mental health solicitor who will be able to assist you with making representations to the tribunal.

✓Your responsible clinician can make a community treatment order (CTO) to give you supervised treatment in the community. While they have the power to do this if you are on a Section 3, they do not if you are on a Section 2, 4 or 5. A CTO means that, instead of staying in hospital to be treated for your mental health problem, you can be treated in the community. Nonetheless, you can be recalled to hospital by your responsible clinician if they believe that both of the following apply: that you require medical treatment in hospital for your mental disorder *and* there would be risk of harm to your health or safety or to others' if you are not recalled. CTOs last 6 months but can be renewed by your responsible clinician. You can apply to the Mental Health Tribunal if you want to be discharged from your CTO. Every CTO will have two conditions – namely, to make yourself available to see your responsible clinician if your CTO is going to be renewed, and that you must see the second opinion appointed doctor if you are asked to. Other conditions can also be added, such as being tested for drugs. You have the right to support from an IMHA while on a CTO.

6

Money

Money is one of those subjects often left out of 'polite' conversation. We're taught maths in school, but not about payday loans, or what to do if our mate has 'forgotten' about the £30 we lent him at the weekend. Just the idea of checking our bank account can feel like a step too far for some of us. Everything 'money' can at times feel awkward, shrouded in embarrassment or resentment; when we find ourselves in difficulties, it can be hard to know what to do.

This chapter won't tell you how to spend, save or budget, but it does aim to give you a sense of your rights in relation to your money, specifically when you are lending it to others, or borrowing it yourself.

Knowing your rights around money is more important than ever. The ability to buy an item by hovering your iPhone over a debit card reader, or just pressing your thumbprint on the home button, adds a new immediacy to the way we can spend and transfer money to others. When it's so easy to spend money, it should be easy to access the laws that protect us – that help us recoup our money, and protect us if we've overstretched ourselves or are struggling.

This chapter is all about how you can lend money safely, what you can do if you don't get your money back, and practical ways you can rely on the law in otherwise casual dealings with friends when it comes to money. It also deals with ways to protect your money, and points to consider if you are dealing with debt.

Lending to friends and family

Having set up a swanky new photography studio, your friend Delphine has her first client booked in for tomorrow morning. At the last minute, her camera breaks and she needs money to fix it. After careful thought, you decide you can afford it for the moment, and she'll pay you back when the studio is up and running … Delphine then falls out with you and you hear nothing further about your money. You contact her 3 months later and she acts as if she has completely forgotten. Not a great situation to be in.

What do you need to know when lending money to friends and family?

Lending money safely

Accurately recording the fact that the money you are giving to another is a loan is nearly always the best way to limit issues arising down the line.

So, from a legal perspective, whenever you lend somebody money, you should have in your mind the question: 'If I end up having to take this person to court to get my money back, what steps can I take *right now* that will help me evidence to a court that the money I gave to the person was a loan, not a gift?'

In other words, how can you prove that you expected to get the money back?

As we know, courts deal with *evidence*. Therefore, when lending money to somebody, you can't really beat a written agreement.

At a basic level, terms for the loan agreement should include the following:

- the amount borrowed
- any interest rate you will be charging (you may choose not to do this with friends)
- repayment terms (for example, 'to be repaid in monthly instalments of £x for 6 months' or 'for the full amount to be repaid on [date]')
- the agreement should also state the consequences of failure to pay – for example that you will 'pursue legal action'

But of course, when lending money to friends or family, a written agreement might not feel like an option, whether because it's too formal or you're afraid to seem ungenerous. Even if a written agreement is the ideal in the eyes of the law, there are other ways to prove your point. Think outside the box. Do you have any other evidence that might be helpful to the court? This could include:

- texts, emails or social media messages discussing the loan with the person or with somebody else
- proof that you initially transferred the money, such as a bank statement
- proof that the money you had given was being repaid as arranged, but then these repayments stopped

✓ If transferring the money online, make use of the reference box. Entitle the transfer of money as 'LOAN' or even 'LOAN – due [date]'. We're often quite prudish when it comes to money, but you shouldn't feel rude stating in the reference box when the money is due to be returned to you. Not only does it help for your own financial planning purposes by enabling you to see at a glance when you can expect the money back, but it is also helpful evidence if matters go to court. The larger the amount of money, the more important this is.

✓ There is an outdated legal principle known as the 'presumption of advancement'. This, broadly speaking, states that if a man transfers property or money to his fiancée or wife, or if a parent transfers property or money to a child, the transfer will be deemed to be a gift, as opposed to a loan, unless there is evidence to the contrary. The presumption of advancement is due to be abolished but, at the time of writing, has not been. It is therefore a factor you should bear in mind, but as this section makes clear, having evidence is the best way to avoid issues.

Court action

If you're reading this part, things are clearly serious. As a general rule, court action should be used as a last resort, so first consider a firm reminder, whether some other form of arrangement can be made, or even mediation.

Mediation

There can be more chance of saving a friendship going down the mediation route compared to the court route. See p. 266 for more information.

Writing a 'letter before claim'

If court is still very much on your mind, you should write the person a 'last chance letter'. This is known as a 'letter before claim'. This is the letter you write to the individual before you start court proceedings.

In the letter, you want to:

- provide the person with a summary of the loan amount, when the loan was given, and when the loan should have been repaid
- inform them that if they do not pay you will be issuing county court proceedings
- give them a reasonable period of time to repay the money

Letters like this can be effective as they show the other person that you are serious. Stating a realistic period of time is also important. It is less about scaring the other person, and more about actually getting your money back!

✓An internet search of 'letter before claim' will help you find some useful templates. As with most things in this book, you may also wish to contact a solicitor specialising in the area.

Final considerations

If all else has failed, court action may feel like the only way forward. It will likely be a consideration you have had all along, but you must ask yourself, honestly, does the person actually have the money to pay you back?

If they do not, it is worth questioning whether it is worth taking the case to court. While our law is many things, it can't give to you something that the person doesn't have themselves. As will be seen in the later chapter on going to court, issuing a claim at court costs *you* money. Is it worth it? A quick internet search will bring up a gov.uk website where you can see the court fees associated with a 'claim for money' (which is the type of claim you would be making).

Borrowing money

So you need a little extra cash. Maybe to pay for a holiday, or maybe to see you through until your next pay day. It is likely that you will consider one of the following:

1. using your credit card
2. a personal loan from your bank or building society
3. a payday loan

The world of credit and loans can be murky and confusing. This chapter won't go into all the details (there are other books for that), but does aim to demystify it slightly, and highlight the rights and protections you have, even in situations where your power feels as precarious as your bank balance.

Credit cards

Credit cards are used for a variety of reasons: they can help to spread out expenses month by month, and can also assist you in building up your credit rating. But it is important to also be aware of the risks. If you are unable to pay what you owe you could quickly accrue debt and open yourself up to fees and charges if you exceed your credit limit. While credit cards can help you build your credit rating, they can also have a negative impact on it if payments are missed.

In terms of the law, when it comes to credit cards, a brilliant piece of legislation you should know about is Section 75 of the Consumer Credit Act 1974. It's pieces of legislation like this that are one of the reasons why I wrote this book. Section 75 aims at ensuring that you don't find yourself paying off a debt for something you never actually received, or you did receive, but was not as it should have been.

What does Section 75 say? While it is never easy to truncate convoluted legislation into one sentence, here is an attempt:

If you buy something on your credit card costing more than £100 and up to £30,000, then the credit card provider is equally as liable as the supplier (seller) if something goes wrong.

The first time many people read about this, they often think that it is too good to be true. It really is a golden piece of legislation. Let's break down what exactly this means.

Let's say you purchase a one-way ticket to Miami directly from SunnySkiesAirways. The ticket costs £400. SunnySkies-Airways then goes bust, nobody hears from them again, and your trip does not take place. You need not fear! You can go to the *credit card company* to get the full amount back.

Now that I have your attention: let me tell you a few more things you ought to know about Section 75 so you can ensure you can benefit from it.

- The amount of the product must be **over** £100. That means you won't qualify if the product costs exactly £100.
- Let's say you order a product for £99 + a £5 delivery charge; although the total cost is over £100, you cannot benefit from Section 75, as the item you bought was under £100.
- Let's say you are going on your long-awaited trip to Rome, and tickets are £60 each way: technically you will not be protected by Section 75 as no single item cost over £100 (even though the combined cost of the tickets did). If, however, you purchased a return ticket that cost £120 – you would be covered.
- To benefit from Section 75 protection, you don't actually have to pay the full amount on your credit card – just part will be sufficient. For example, let's say an item you pay

for is £500 and you pay a £50 deposit on your credit card for it – this is enough to give you the full protection, even if you use another means of payment for the outstanding £450.

✓ Section 75 only applies to credit cards. If you made a purchase using a debit card, look into the 'chargeback' scheme offered by many debit card providers which operates in a similar way.

Personal loans

A personal loan is where you borrow a lump sum of money from the bank and then pay it back, usually in fixed instalments each month. Many people are fond of them as when it comes to larger amounts of money, banks often charge a lower rate of interest than they do on credit cards.

The financial organisations listed within the Useful Organisations section (from p. 277) are better placed than I am to give information in this regard, but here are a few things that you need to know ASAP, as it's frankly scandalous that they weren't taught to you in school.

1. **You won't necessarily receive the APR advertised.** Whenever a loan (or credit card) is advertised, the annual percentage rate (APR) must be shown. The APR refers to the total cost of borrowing money for a year. It includes the interest you'll have to pay and any fees that are automatically included, such as an application fee or annual fee. All lenders calculate APR the same way, which makes it easier for you to compare them. The *key thing to remember*

is that when you are shopping around for a loan or a credit card, the APR you will see advertised *is not necessarily the APR that you, personally, will get*. The APRs advertised are known as 'representative' APRs. This means that at least 51 per cent of customers receive a rate that is equal to this, or lower. While this assists in allowing you to compare loans, the reality is that you may find that the personal APR that you are offered by the bank or company is very different to the representative APR. For example, it could be much higher if you have a poor credit history.

2. **Be aware of 'secured loans'.** If you enter the bank looking for a loan and also own your own home, it may be suggested to you that you consider taking out a secured loan. These loans are known as 'secured' because the bank will require something as 'security' in case you cannot pay the loan back. This might seem an attractive option as the interest rates tend to be lower, but if you can't pay back the money, the bank can apply to the courts and force you to sell your home to pay off the money you owe.

3. **Early repayment penalties.** Conventional wisdom would suggest it is always a good idea to pay off a loan as quickly as you can. If you plan to do this, first carefully read the terms in your loan agreement. Some lenders will charge you a penalty for paying off the loan early. Therefore, before you take out a loan, if you suspect you may be able to pay it off early, consider going for a loan that does not penalise you for doing so.

✓ Always read the small print. Ensure you understand everything mentioned. Ask questions of the lender if you don't. We all feel embarrassed asking silly questions – but remember, there is no such thing as a silly question when your signature is involved.

Payday loans

Thinking of taking out a payday loan? What rights you have, and what legal requirements will be attached to repayments, will depend on the wording of the loan – so make sure you look a little wider than going for what just at first glance appears to be the best deal.

These are some handy protections you should know about:

- Interest on payday loans is capped at 0.8 per cent per day.
- You should *never* have to pay back more than twice what you borrowed.
- If you take a loan out for 30 days, you should be charged no more in fees and charges than £24 for every £100 borrowed. If you don't pay it back on time, the most you can be charged in 'default fees' is £15 plus interest on the amount borrowed.
- When you take out a payday loan, in most instances, you will pay the lender back by enabling them to take the money out of your account (a bit like a direct debit). This is called a Continuous Payment Authority (CPA). **It is your legal right to cancel the CPA, even if the payday loan company refuses. The bank must cancel it for you.**

However, obviously it is important to then find another way to pay what you owe – otherwise, more problems will arise!

Some positive steps all payday lenders must take:

- They should check whether you'll be able to pay back the money before lending it to you; for example, via proof of income.
- All of their adverts must include the warning: 'Late repayment can cause you serious money problems. For help, go to www.moneyadviceservice.org.uk.'
- The main features of the loan should be explained to you. You should know how much you will need to pay back and the consequences if you don't, as well as be informed that you will be charged extra for late payment and that the loan is not suitable for long-term borrowing.
- They should explain to you how CPAs work, and how to cancel them.

If any of the above has not been done, you may want to consider making a complaint to the Financial Ombudsman Service (FOS). Turn to p. 277 for details on organisations that can provide greater assistance with this.

Struggling with debt

Somehow debt remains an uncomfortable topic to talk about – despite so much of the population being in some form of it. If you are struggling with debt, the debt advice organisations listed in the back of the book will be well placed to give advice specific to your circumstances. The information contained within this section is to give you an awareness of just some of the options that are available to you.

If you are facing financial difficulty, there may be good reason to let your creditor know. A number of Codes of Practice in the credit industry state that if an individual informs them that they are in financial difficulty, the creditor should give consideration to reducing the interest and any charges they pay. It is also worth knowing that you may be able to get something called 'breathing space' while you deal with your debts. The organisations listed at the back of the book are best placed to advise on how breathing space might work in your circumstances, but if you are able to access it, it can result in there being a temporary halting of phone calls and letters from your creditor, and also a pause in certain interest fees, penalties, charges and any enforcement action to recover the debt.

If you are vulnerable or somebody who may find it more challenging to deal with your debts, whether that be due to, for example, a recent relationship breakdown, recent bereavement or a mental health difficulty, you may find that you are able to change the way your creditors interact with you by informing them of this. Creditors will often have staff specially trained in liaising with people who are vulnerable. This change in approach could help alleviate some of the anxiety that comes from communicating with your creditors. Your creditor will need to know of your vulnerabilities in order to do this, and it may even be that they can accommodate you in some way, for example by giving you a short break from payments. Speak to the relevant organisations listed in the back of the book for advice on how you can move forward if you are considering talking to your creditor about circumstances that may make dealing with your debts more challenging.

If you plan to make a complaint to a creditor, it may be helpful to turn to Chapter 12 for handy pointers on how you can structure your letter (if you choose to make your complaint in writing, which is recommended).

Enforcement agents (bailiffs)

You see what you believe to be bailiffs walking up your driveway. In that moment, you realise just how little you know when it comes to their powers.

Key things to know

The following information applies to bailiffs visiting your home in relation to a consumer credit debt – for example debt arising from a credit card or personal loan.

The most important thing to note is that bailiffs can only come into the picture if the creditor has obtained a County Court Judgment (CCJ) against you. If they have not obtained a CCJ, you *should not* be receiving a visit from a bailiff. On top of this, a bailiff will appear only if you have been ordered to pay an amount by the court and didn't pay it by the due date. This is because if you have a CCJ and do not pay as the court has ordered, the creditor is able to make an application to the court for something called a 'warrant of control'. This is what gives the bailiff authorisation to come to your home in an effort to take control of your possessions.

People commonly mistake a 'debt collector' for a bailiff, but they are entirely distinct. If a debt collector visits your home, they have to leave if you ask them to, as they do not have the same powers as bailiffs.

What happens if bailiffs enter your property?

If bailiffs do get into your property, they will make an inventory of the goods they can take and ask that you sign it – this is known as a controlled goods agreement. This gives them the right to return at a later date to take the goods, and they can use reasonable force to enter. If you refuse to sign they have the right to remove the goods immediately.

Bailiffs can't take:

- essential domestic goods (e.g. beds and bedding)
- goods that are owned entirely by someone else or subject to hire purchase or bill of sale
- goods with no resale value
- goods that are fixed to your property (e.g. fitted wardrobes)

In all cases, ask for ID – don't assume they are a bailiff just because they say they are.

✓ If you have a car outside your home, bailiffs can take the car without getting into your home.

✓ In the context being discussed here, bailiffs cannot force entry. Therefore, if you do not want to let a bailiff in – do not open your door. It is nonetheless worth knowing that in some contexts, they may, technically, be able to use 'reasonable force' to access your property. This could be if the matter is in relation to court fines, HMRC tax debts or if you have broken a controlled goods agreement. Reasonable force would not entitle them to kick your door down, but rather more along the lines of them using a locksmith.

7

Employment

If you are spending half your waking hours in an office building, you ought to know the rights you have while there. Actually, in the pursuit of giving you good bang for your buck, this chapter will also tell you about the rights relating to your employment when you *aren't* there – from when you are on annual leave, to when you are out of work due to pregnancy. It will also cover individuals who might not go into an office at all, such as freelancers.

Within nearly any employment context, there will be 'office politics' and personal relationships to think about. This book cannot give you guidance there. You may, for example, know that you are being asked to work over and above that which you are contractually required to, but choose to let this slide in an effort to be perceived as a hard worker and increase your prospects of promotion. These are considerations for you to make and this book passes no judgement. This chapter will just ensure that, whatever decision you make, you are aware of the law that sits behind it.

As employees we are all used to working to deadlines. The most important thing you need to be aware of if things go wrong at work is that there is also a deadline for taking legal action against your employer. This chapter will inform you of these deadlines so you aren't caught on the back foot.

Even if you are happy at work, feel valued and fulfilled, remember that in the private sector your job is to create profit for the organisation – and at the end of the day, no number of office perks will make up for being exploited, save you when the numbers get tight, or protect you when new management comes in and they want to unfairly get rid of you. What can give you protection is knowing your rights.

Employment status

Going to work. Yawn. Before we delve into what your rights are, we need to figure out what *type* of 'worker' you are. No – not a 'hard worker', as you may have said on your CV, but your employment status.

There are three main categories:

- an employee
- a worker
- self-employed

Employee: An employee is an individual who has entered into or works under a contract of employment. They might work, say, 4 or 5 days a week. They may just work for one employer and, while at work, their boss has a certain level of control over their day-to-day actions (the level of control will vary depending on the nature of the role). They are personally obliged to do work, and in turn their employer is obliged to pay them. They typically couldn't, for example, pass their work on to somebody else.

Worker: The way in which a 'worker' works is often more casual. They will often have a contract stating they are to do work 'as and when required'. There is little obligation on the company to provide them with work and little obligation on the worker to accept it. Short-term casual workers, along with agency workers who are not employed by their agency, are likely to be workers.

Self-employed: Self-employed people work for themselves. They will typically get contracts to provide services for clients and will choose when and how they work. They invoice for their pay and, where appropriate, can delegate somebody else to do the work. Freelancers will very often be classed as self-employed.

Zero-hour contracts

Zero-hour contract workers will most likely be 'workers' but could also be employees. What your employment status is will depend on what is stated in your contract and how, in practice, the arrangement operates.

Agency workers

If you are an agency worker, you should be aware that you have rights on your first day, but also additional rights that kick in once you have worked in the same job (known as the 'hiring organisation' – for example, the call centre you're working at) for 12 weeks. The rights you will have straight away include: being paid at least the minimum wage, being protected from discrimination, and being informed of relevant vacancies in the hiring organisation. Your rights after 12 weeks include rights relating to pensions, sick leave and parental leave. As for the employment status of an agency worker, there usually will be no direct contract between yourself and the hiring organisation. You will usually have a contract with the agency, and the agency a contract with the hiring organisation. You potentially could be either a worker or an employee of the agency. The nature of the working relationship, the terms of your contract and the legal tests discussed below can help ascertain this.

The legal tests for employment status

As a rule of thumb, the following legal tests can be kept in mind when ascertaining whether you are an employee, worker or self-employed. These are: 'personal service', 'mutuality of obligation' and 'control'.

- Personal service means that you personally agree to do the work or service and can't send a substitute.

- Mutuality of obligation tends to mean that the supplier of work is obliged to provide you with work, and you are obliged to accept this work in return for being paid.
- Control means that the supplier of work has the power to determine what, where, when and how the work is done.

You are likely to be an employee if: there is an obligation on you to provide personal service, there is mutuality of obligation, and the supplier of the work controls how the work is done.

You are likely to be a worker if: there is an obligation on you to provide personal service, there is mutuality of obligation, the other party is not a customer for the business you are carrying out and you don't meet the test for being an employee (i.e. you do not work under a contract of employment).

You are likely to be self-employed if: there is no obligation on you to provide personal service, or there is no mutuality of obligation, or the other party is the customer for the business you are carrying out.

Final note

It is important to stress that just because (for example) your written contract states that you have a certain type of employment status, this is not conclusive of the actual relationship between you and the person/organisation providing you with work. A person's actual employment status can at times be a complex legal question and many factors will be considered – such as whether the work given to an individual must be accepted by them, and whether the work needing to be done can be completed by a substitute.

The 2021 Uber case demonstrates just how important this all is. The taxi-hailing and delivery organisation claimed that their drivers were self-employed; however, the court found that they were in fact workers – entitling them to a number of rights such as paid annual leave and the National Minimum/ Living Wage (things they would not have been entitled to if they were self-employed). A number of factors were taken into account by the court – such as the fact that Uber set the terms of the contract and drivers had no say in them, and the fact that drivers could be penalised if they rejected too many rides.

Pay

This section will focus on employees and workers.

National Minimum Wage and National Living Wage

There is a minimum amount that you *must* be paid for the hours that you work. The rates are increased by the government from April each year. If you are an employee or worker, you *must* receive the National Minimum Wage (or National Living Wage if aged 23 or over). From 1 April 2021, the rates are as follows.

aged 23 or over (National Living Wage) – £8.91
aged 21 to 22 – £8.36
aged 18 to 20 – £6.56
under 18 – £4.62
apprentice – £4.30

✓You may have heard of the London Living Wage. This is an hourly rate of pay that reflects the higher cost of living in London and is calculated independently. The London Living Wage is not mandatory. In other words, you are not legally entitled to receive this wage solely based on the fact that you work in London. At the time of writing, the London Living Wage is £10.85 per hour.

✓If you work in the services/hospitality industry, be aware that tips and gratuities do not count towards minimum wage. Don't allow your employer to suggest otherwise. Tips should be on top of your hourly wage. If you work in sales, you should know that commission *does* count towards minimum wage. If the amount of commission you have received is too low to meet the minimum wage, your employer should make up the difference by 'topping up' your pay.

If you suspect you are not receiving the National Minimum Wage or National Living Wage

By law, you should be receiving the National Minimum Wage (or National Living Wage if aged 23 or over). If you suspect that you are not, you should first check that this is the case. Use the 'National Minimum Wage and Living Wage calculator' on the gov.uk website. Some deductions can lawfully be made from your pay that may take you under the National

Minimum Wage or National Living Wage, such as tax and National Insurance contributions.

If, having used the calculator, you still do not believe you are receiving what you are entitled to, you may want to query this with your employer. See p. 264 for some helpful pointers on how to have a good conversation with somebody in authority.

If the issue cannot be resolved informally, you may wish to consider making a formal complaint to your employer – known as 'raising a grievance' (discussed later in this chapter).

You could also make a claim to an employment tribunal. The most important thing to know at this stage is that you must make your claim to an employment tribunal within 3 months. This is known as the 'limitation date'. Employment tribunals are independent tribunals with authority to make decisions about employment disputes.

Annual leave ('holiday')

Calculating how much you are entitled to

When it comes to holidays, the magic number is 5.6. By law, you are entitled to 5.6 weeks' paid holiday each year (known as 'statutory annual leave' – note that an employer can include bank holidays as part of statutory annual leave). For a basic calculation of how many days this means you can take away from your office desk, multiply the number of days you work each week by 5.6.

So, if you work 5 days a week, you are legally entitled to 28 days' paid holiday each year. Remember, this is the legal minimum – some employers will give their employees more than this.

If you don't work the conventional 5 days a week it can get tricky to calculate your annual leave entitlement. Don't leave it to your employer to figure this out – you need to know it yourself.

If you work, say, 3 days a week, you're entitled to 16.8 days' paid holiday (3 × 5.6) each year. Remember, you just need to multiply the number of days you work each week by 5.6.

✓ If your employer gives all of her full-time employees 6 weeks' paid holiday each year (so 30 days instead of the statutory 28 days), you must proportionally get the same, even if you work part time. So, if you work 2 days a week, you should receive 12 days' paid holiday instead of 11.2.

Zero-hour contracts or irregular work

It is important to remember that even if you work irregular work (such as on a zero-hour contract or do shift work), you are still entitled to the legal minimum of 5.6 weeks.

Calculating your holiday is a little more complex in these situations, where on some weeks you may work 5 days and others go without working any days (or hours) at all. Fortunately, help is at hand – search 'holiday entitlement calculator' on the internet and click the link directing you to the gov.uk website, which, depending on your precise circumstances, may be able to assist.

Other things to know when it comes to annual leave

Check your contract to see if your annual leave 'carries over' to the following year if you don't use it. If it does not – go and book some annual leave! If you are in a job and you feel you literally cannot take annual leave, perhaps because the project you are engrossed in is so important, have a frank chat with your boss explaining this and see if an agreement can be reached. What you want to avoid is using your annual leave to work from your kitchen table as opposed to your office one.

If you have already used all of your paid holiday, or want some time off but don't want to use up your paid holiday, you could consider asking for unpaid leave. Information on how to request unpaid leave is sometimes set out in your contract, but if not, have a chat with your boss and see if an agreement can be reached. Remember – address this smartly. Don't let it just be about you, but also think about the company. Are there any steps you can take to persuade the employer that your absence won't be felt too significantly? Can you obtain the confirmation of your colleagues that they have the capacity to cover your work before you have a chat with your boss?

✓ It's commonly accepted that a way to progress at work is to be 'first one in, last one out'. It is your choice to do this – but, particularly if you have this mentality, I would encourage you to keep the same spirit when it comes to taking your holiday. Burnout is real, and, all too often, you are replaceable. Keep yourself healthy!

Being ill

The other big topic we need to talk about is sick pay. Employees are entitled to this and workers are too if they meet eligibility conditions.

When you are sick, your bills still need to be paid. So what happens in relation to your income?

The moment you feel that sniffle coming on, along with grabbing tissues, grab your employment contract. You want to see if there are any particular rules your employer has when it comes to sick pay, but also, how much you will be paid and how long it will last.

Irrespective of what is said in your contract, it is important you know what the law is here. In short, there are minimum requirements that your employer *must* meet when it comes to sick pay, provided you meet the eligibility. They must pay you what is called 'Statutory Sick Pay' (SSP). For these requirements to kick in, the following must have taken place:

- You have been off sick for a minimum of 4 days in a row (this includes non-working days).
- When averaged out, you earn at least the lower earnings limit (LEL), which at the time of writing is £120 per week (this is before tax – not take-home pay).
- You have confirmed your illness in writing to your employer within 7 days (or any deadline your employer has set).

SSP is £96.35 a week at the time of writing. It is paid from the 4th day of sickness and can be paid for up to 28 weeks.

Remember – these are *minimum* requirements. Many employers will in fact pay you sick pay from the 1st day you are off sick as opposed to the 4th.

Taking annual leave while off sick

While you are off sick, you *can* take holiday. This might be done where, while you are physically unable to work, you are physically able to take a holiday. It may also be done where you are off sick for a long period of time or due to a mental health condition and having a holiday may assist you in your recovery. The ball is in your court to ask your employer for holiday while off sick. If your employer says yes, your sick leave can be paused and you should get your normal holiday pay while on holiday. If after you have taken your holiday you are still ill and unfit to return to work, your sick pay can continue.

Getting sick while on holiday

What about the dreaded nightmare? Your holiday to Jamaica is booked, and just as you're leaving for the airport, you develop a headache. Next thing you know you're bed-bound in Croydon, about as far from Jamaica as possible, with a nasty fever and a doctor's note telling you not to leave the house for at least a week.

If this happens to you, and you want to take some / all of your holiday as sick leave, you must let your employer know.

You can then take your holiday as sick leave instead, meaning you can use the holiday for another time. Your holiday entitlement accrues as normal while you are off sick.

If due to being on long-term sick leave you have not been able to use your holiday in a given year, up to 4 weeks' unused holiday can be carried over. Your employer may allow more than 4 weeks, so check your employment contract. You have 18 months to use the holiday from the date it is carried over.

Having a baby

Everything surrounding the arrival of a new baby can be incredibly exciting. Learning about the accompanying work-related laws, on the other hand, is not. This section hopes to make this mundane (but very important) information that bit more palatable.

Maternity leave

You have to be an **employee** to qualify for maternity leave. You have the right to up to 52 weeks' maternity leave. This right exists from the first day of starting your job – you don't need to worry about having accrued enough working days.

You can work right up to giving birth, or you can start your maternity leave from up to 11 weeks before your baby is due – the choice is yours. Nonetheless, when your baby is born, you *must* take at least 2 weeks off (or 4 weeks if you are a factory worker).

If you decide to work right up to giving birth, as mentioned earlier, you *must* start your maternity leave when your baby is born and must also take it all in one go. Employees can carry out up to 10 days' work – known as 'keeping in touch' (KIT) days – for their employer during their maternity leave without bringing the maternity leave to an end (see further discussion on KIT days below). With that exception, when you go back to work (even if you have not used all of the 52 weeks), your maternity leave and pay ends.

If, in the 4 weeks before your baby is due, you need to go off work due to pregnancy-related illness, your maternity leave will start automatically (unless you and your employer agree that it should be delayed).

If your baby arrives earlier than expected, your maternity leave will start straight away and your employer will need to be informed as soon as possible. Somebody else can do this on your behalf if necessary. After all, you will have more important things on. If your baby arrives late, you can still start your maternity leave from the date you had previously told your employer. Nonetheless, be sure to inform your employer when your baby is born so that your compulsory maternity leave is able to start.

If you experience a miscarriage or stillbirth after the 24th week of pregnancy, or your baby passes away shortly after being born at any stage of pregnancy, you are still entitled to maternity pay and leave. If you experience a miscarriage or stillbirth before the 24th week, you may wish to speak to your employer to see if they can offer you other support.

Maternity pay

Maternity leave and maternity pay are distinct. Some people are entitled to maternity pay when they go on maternity leave; others are not. A key term to know is 'qualifying week'. Your qualifying week is calculated by counting 15 weeks back from the week you are due to have your baby.

You may be entitled to Statutory Maternity Pay (SMP). The eligibility criteria is as follows:

- You have worked continuously for the same employer for 26 weeks before your qualifying week.
- You earn at least £120 a week (the LEL). (If your earnings vary, it will need to be the case that you earned at least £120 a week on average for the 8 weeks before your qualifying week.)
- You are still pregnant 11 weeks before the week in which it is expected that childbirth will occur.
- You give the employer at least 28 days' notice of the date you intend the maternity leave to start (or, if that is not reasonably practicable, as much notice as is).
- You have ceased working.

SMP is paid for up to 39 weeks. For the first 6 weeks you will get 90 per cent of your average weekly earnings, and for the following 33 weeks you will get either a prescribed weekly rate which is set by the government each tax year (currently £151.97) or 90 per cent of your average weekly earnings (whichever is lower).

You may have spotted that while maternity leave is up to 52 weeks, SMP is only up to 39 weeks, which means that the last 13 weeks are unpaid. It is worth remembering that we are talking about statutory maternity pay – in other words, the legal minimum. Your employer may offer you more money than the legal minimum, or maternity pay for a longer period than the legal minimum. Have a chat with them or review your employment contract for information about this.

Paternity leave

To be eligible for paternity leave, the following must apply:

- You have been in continuous employment with your employer for 26 weeks up to any day in the qualifying week.
- You have (or expect to have) responsibility for a child's upbringing, and are either the biological father to a child or the partner to someone who is having a baby.
- You must not have already taken shared parental leave in respect of the same child.

If these factors apply, you can choose to take either 1 or 2 weeks of paternity leave.

You can start your paternity leave from the day the child is born (but not before) or from an agreed date within 56 days of the child's birth. Your leave must be taken in one go and must end within 56 days of the child being born.

You will need to inform your employer that you plan to

take paternity leave by the end of the 15th week before the baby is expected. You must let them know how much leave you will be taking, the week the baby is due, and the date you will start your leave.

✓ If you are an employee, you have the right to unpaid time off to attend two antenatal appointments with your partner. You can take 6.5 hours per appointment. Of course, if your employer consents, you can take more time than this (or use some of your holiday to cover the gap between the amount of time you have a right to and amount of time you wish to take).

Paternity pay

Paternity pay is at the same rate as maternity pay. The eligibility is the same too. See the 'Maternity pay' section above.

Shared parental leave

You may want to look into something called shared parental leave. This gives greater flexibility in terms of how you and your partner can care for the new addition to your family and, importantly, helps ensure that there is still parental care when the mother returns to work. In order to be eligible, the mother and partner must have been in continuous employment with their employers for at least 26 weeks up to the qualifying week. There is quite a bit to know about shared parental leave, more than this book can cover. If it sounds like an option of interest to you, do your own research, and speak to your line manager or HR department.

✓ If you are in a same-sex relationship, one of you can take paternity leave and the other maternity leave or adoption leave. Helpful information on adoption leave is available on the Acas website (the Advisory, Conciliation and Arbitration Service: see p. 277), if this is of interest to you.

When should I tell my employer I am pregnant?

You must tell your employer that you are pregnant at least 15 weeks before your baby is due if you are entitled to paid maternity leave (if this is not possible, perhaps because you were unaware you were pregnant, then as soon as possible). If you think '4 months before' in your head, you will be sufficiently covered. You must also tell them on what week your baby is due and when you want to start maternity leave. Your employer can ask to see proof of your pregnancy and due date such as a letter from your doctor or midwife, or the MAT B1 Certificate – a certificate you will receive not more than 20 weeks before the expected week of childbirth.

Your employer will need to reply to you within 28 days, confirming the date your maternity leave will run to. This should be in writing. If it is not, it is sensible to request it.

Always remember: when applying for a job, you do not need to inform the employer that you are pregnant. If you choose to, they legally cannot use the pregnancy as a reason for rejecting you or otherwise treat you unfavourably because of your pregnancy.

Logistical matters

Your doctor may advise you to attend appointments before you have your baby (antenatal appointments). These may include going for scans and pregnancy health checks, or going to pregnancy/parent-related classes. You have the legal right to reasonable time off with full pay in order for you to attend these appointments, regardless of whether you work full time or part time. If you are an **agency worker**, provided you have worked at least 12 continuous weeks in the same job, you can get paid time off for antenatal appointments.

If your job contains a health and safety risk to you or your unborn baby, the risk must be removed by your employer. Risks might centre around the fact that your job involves, for example, heavy lifting, exposure to certain chemicals, or being on your feet and active for prolonged periods of time. A solution for you and your employer may be altering your working conditions or duties so you are not put at any risk, or your employer changing your job to something completely different that does not pose a risk to you or your unborn baby. Even if your job needs to be temporarily changed, the terms of your contract should not, so you need not worry about a reduction in pay.

Sometimes it might not be possible for your employer to remove the risk. This isn't your problem – it is your employer's. The law does not require you to persevere and put yourself and your unborn baby at risk. In such a situation, your employer may suspend you on full pay. This may be for the period of time while the risk at work is still present, or until your maternity leave starts. Your suspension on full pay will automatically switch to maternity pay and leave once you enter the 4th week before you are due to give birth.

If you work for an agency, they have the responsibility in this area (provided you have worked at least 12 continuous weeks in the same job). If the job is not suitable while you are pregnant, your agency should put you forward for suitable alternative work. If no such alternative work is available, they should give you paid time off for at least the length of the original assignment. If you are deemed to have unreasonably refused suitable work, the agency does not need to pay you anything.

If you love your workplace too much to be away, thanks to something called 'keeping in touch' days, you don't have to. Keeping in touch days mean you can work up to 10 days during your maternity leave. These are optional, in that both you and your employer need to agree to them. It is for you to agree with your employer how many of these days you will work, what type of work you will do and how much you will be paid.

✓**IVF pregnancies:** Once you reach the last part of the IVF process, namely the embryo transfer stage, your pregnancy rights will come into force. You have the same pregnancy and maternity rights as with non-IVF pregnancies. For more information, visit the Acas website (see p. 277).

Returning to your old job once your baby is born

If you have taken 26 weeks' or less maternity leave, you have the legal right to return to the same job. The terms of the job (e.g. pay) cannot be any worse than when you left. Simple.

If you have taken more than 26 weeks' maternity leave, while you have the right to return to the same job, if this is not possible you can be offered a similar job. A huge change having taken place in the organisation while you were away may be an example of a circumstance that means having your old job back is not possible. The similar job must not have worse conditions or pay than your previous one.

If you want to return to work earlier or later than you had originally told your employer, ensure that you inform them at least 8 weeks before the date you are due to return to work.

Important legal protections in relation to maternity

It is illegal for an employer to make you redundant because you are pregnant or on maternity leave. This is automatically unfair dismissal (see p. 191). You could also make a separate claim for discrimination (see below).

Receiving bad treatment at work

Being treated unfairly at work never feels nice. It can also lead to your performance slipping, causing other issues. Often in life, it is the absence of a solution that exacerbates our grief.

This section aims to give you some remedies and routes you may wish to consider exploring.

For a moment, let's step away from the emotion and consider your treatment through the prism of the law. The actions you can consider will depend on what the treatment is classed as. Generally speaking, your treatment will fall into (at least) one of the following categories: bullying, harassment, discrimination or victimisation. I will spend some time discussing each – read them all and see which one fits your experience.

Bullying

Bullying is unwanted behaviour from an individual or group that makes you feel uncomfortable. It can take many different forms. It could, for example, be things such as colleagues spreading rumours about you, your boss giving you more work than others, being blocked from promotional opportunities, or being talked down to at meetings. Incidents outside of the office environment can also count, such as on social media or at an office party. It could be just one incident, or something recurring.

If your workplace has a policy on bullying, this will help you to understand how complaints of bullying should be handled. Be aware that regardless of whether or not there is a policy, while you are at work your employer has a legal duty of care to protect you, which includes dealing with bullying.

A claim for constructive unfair dismissal (see p. 192) could be made to an employment tribunal if your employer does nothing about severe bullying that causes you to have to leave your job.

Odd as it may seem, bullying is not necessarily against the law. Nonetheless, if the unwanted behaviour is related to something such as your gender or race, the behaviour may constitute harassment, which *is* against the law.

Harassment

As touched on in Chapter 3, the Equality Act 2010 lays out a number of 'protected characteristics' which also have application in the context of the workplace. If unwanted behaviour (which may include bullying) is due to any of the following protected characteristics, it will amount to harassment:

- age
- disability
- gender reassignment
- race
- religion or belief
- sex
- sexual orientation

Neither 'marriage and civil partnership' nor 'pregnancy and maternity' are included in this list, as the law on harassment does not cover them. Nonetheless, harassment related to sex or sexual orientation often covers the same behaviour.

For behaviour to amount to harassment, the unwanted

conduct must have the purpose or effect of violating your dignity or creating an intimidating, hostile, degrading, humiliating or offensive environment for you.

Harassment can take many forms in a workplace context – it could be frequent behaviour from someone, or one serious incident. It could even include things that are 'supposed' to be funny, such as pranks or unwanted 'banter'.

The law on harassment applies whether or not you actually have the protected characteristic around which you are being harassed.

If you don't have the protected characteristic yourself, but you witness somebody else being harassed due to their protected characteristic and you are upset by it, this could also constitute harassment of you. In addition, the harassment laws will apply if the harassment is due to you being linked with someone of a protected characteristic – for example, if you have a boyfriend of a certain race and you are receiving unwanted conduct because of his race, this could constitute harassment.

Unwanted behaviour you receive that is of a sexual nature may amount to sexual harassment. This behaviour need not necessarily be physical or verbal, but, among other things, could be something written down or an image drawn.

If your workplace has a policy on discrimination and harassment, this should help you understand how complaints will be dealt with.

Discrimination

Being discriminated against is when you are treated unfairly due to any of the protected characteristics listed in the 'Harassment' section, with the addition of 'marriage and civil partnership', and 'pregnancy and maternity'.

Discrimination can be direct or indirect. This is best illustrated by examples.

Direct discrimination

Person A and Person B are both at the same level at work. Because of Person A's sexual orientation, Person B is offered a promotion over Person A – despite Person A being more qualified for the role.

Of course, it is relatively uncommon for people to state that they have acted in a certain way because of another person's protected characteristic. Therefore, direct discrimination is determined by relying on a 'comparator' who does not share the relevant protected characteristic; this may be an actual person or what is called a 'hypothetical comparator'. In the earlier example, Person B could be the comparator.

The next stage, taking into account that comparator, would be to consider whether there are facts from which you could properly or fairly conclude that the difference in treatment was because of the protected characteristic. If so, the employer would have to show that there was in fact a non-discriminatory reason for the difference in treatment.

If you are treated unfairly because somebody *thinks* you have a certain protected characteristic, even if you actually don't, it's still a type of direct discrimination – this is known as 'perceptive discrimination'. An example would be if somebody were to treat you less favourably because of what they thought your religion was, even though in reality you hold a different religious belief.

At this point it is also worth mentioning 'associative discrimination'. This is where you are treated unfairly because of the protected characteristic of somebody you know or are associated with. Let's say your best friend, who is of Pakistani origin, picks you up from work. If on seeing this your work colleagues treat you less favourably, that would be associative discrimination.

Direct discrimination cannot be justified, except on grounds of age: in these circumstances an employer can treat people of different ages differently provided the difference in treatment can be shown to be a proportionate means of achieving a legitimate aim of the employer. This justification is typically described as 'objective justification' and is relevant to other areas of discrimination law.

Indirect discrimination

Company X has a policy that mandates all staff must work on a Saturday. This causes particular trouble to its employees who are Seventh-day Adventists (a Christian denomination), who believe Saturday is the Sabbath day and as such attend church then.

Indirect discrimination may be a little harder to spot at first glance. It is when a policy/rule/arrangement applies to everybody, but disadvantages those sharing a certain protected characteristic.

A discriminatory policy / rule / arrangement that is applied to everyone, but puts you at a disadvantage, will not amount to indirect discrimination if your employer can show that there is an 'objective justification'. Each case will turn on its facts, but an example might be if you work in a laboratory in a role requiring all persons performing it to have a steady hand due to the hazardous chemicals being handled. If you were to develop a disability giving you a particularly shaky hand, your employer may have an 'objective justification' in no longer allowing you to handle such chemicals.

Disabilities

There are some forms of discrimination that only apply to those with disabilities.

The term 'disability' is defined in the Equality Act 2010. A disabled person is someone who has a physical or mental impairment which has a substantial and long-term adverse effect on their ability to carry out normal day-to-day activities. It can include things like anxiety and depression or a chronic injury. People with HIV, MS or cancer are automatically deemed to be disabled.

It is important to keep the definition in mind, because it may include some people who do not necessarily consider themselves to be disabled.

Your employer must have knowledge of your disability for much of the following information to apply.

Discrimination arising from a disability

This form of discrimination may be found if your employer treats you unfavourably because of something that arises from your disability.

So, to give an example, an employee may be suffering from depression. This may cause them to be constantly tired. This in turn could result in that employee always being late for work. This is something that therefore 'arises' from the disability.

If (using this example) your employer treats you unfavourably because of your lateness and has knowledge of your disability, this will be discrimination unless that treatment can be objectively justified.

Duty to make reasonable adjustments

If a rule or practice of an employer puts a disabled person at a substantial disadvantage compared to a non-disabled person, the employer will be under a duty to take reasonable steps to avoid that disadvantage provided they have knowledge of the disability.

This duty also applies if there is a physical feature at the relevant workplace that puts a disabled person at a substantial disadvantage or if without some specific aid (an auxiliary aid) that person would be put at a substantial disadvantage. In these circumstances the employer would be required to take reasonable steps to avoid the disadvantage or provide the specific aid.

A failure to make reasonable adjustments constitutes discrimination.

Victimisation

Victimisation will include unfair treatment resulting from you having made or supported a complaint to do with a protected characteristic (or somebody thinking you did). The relevant protected characteristics are those listed in the 'Harassment' section on p. 178, in addition to 'marriage and civil partnership', and 'pregnancy and maternity'.

An example might be if your boss says a racial slur to a colleague, that colleague makes a claim against your boss as a result, and you support their claim by giving evidence as a witness. If your boss then starts to treat you unfairly – this may be victimisation.

The treatment you receive can count as victimisation even if you never actually made / supported such a complaint, but an individual mistakenly thinks you did.

Check to see if your workplace has a policy on discrimination and victimisation. If it does, this should detail how such matters should be handled.

✓ At the start of any new job, it's a good idea to scan all of the policy documents into one big PDF and enable text recognition. This means that, whatever issue you have at work, you can use the Ctrl+F function to search for key words and see if there is a policy on the issue. It is much easier to force positive results at work when instead of trying to play to a person's good nature, you can show them a policy they have to follow.

Steps you can take

If, having read the above sections, you wish to take things further, this part is for you. Trying to deal with things informally will typically be the quickest way. You may want to arrange an informal meeting with your employer. If the problem is more serious, raising a grievance (a formal complaint) may be a more appropriate approach. Your workplace should have a grievance policy telling you how to raise a grievance, whom you should send it to and what the procedure will be. The Acas website (see p. 277) contains letter templates that can assist you in the writing of your grievance letter and other relevant information.

If your issue relates to discrimination, harassment or victimisation, you could make a claim to an employment tribunal. Importantly, you have 3 months less 1 day from the date of the act in question to pursue your claim. As with all employment tribunal claims, there are circumstances in which the tribunal can extend time (i.e. where it will accept claims that would normally be considered late or out of time). If you are considering this, google 'making a claim to an employment tribunal' and click on the Acas website link. There are important steps you must take before going to the tribunal which are detailed there.

Dismissal

Dismissal is an area we often try not to think about. 'It can't possibly happen to me,' we tell ourselves. The world of dismissal is one we should all be familiar with. If you find yourself in that world, which can be all-consuming, it is helpful to have a pre-existing basic knowledge of your legal rights and entitlements.

Put simply, dismissal is generally when your employer ends your employment.

Different types of dismissal

Important further detail will follow, but the different types of dismissal can be briefly summarised as follows:

Fair dismissal: A fair dismissal is where your employer has dismissed you due to one of five potentially fair reasons. Your employer must also have acted reasonably and fairly in carrying out the dismissal.

Unfair dismissal: An unfair dismissal is where your contract is terminated without fair reason or where it was not reasonable to dismiss you in the circumstances. It is to be noted that there are specific circumstances whereby, if they amount to the main reason for you being dismissed, the dismissal is automatically classed as unfair.

Constructive unfair dismissal: Constructive unfair dismissal is where your employer has seriously breached your contract of employment and you resign as a result.

Wrongful dismissal: Wrongful dismissal applies where you are dismissed in breach of your contract.

Discriminatory dismissal: Discriminatory dismissal applies where you have been dismissed for a discriminatory reason.

Fair dismissal

There are occasions when an employer can dismiss you fairly, and other times when they cannot. Your employer must follow a fair procedure.

The five reasons you can potentially be dismissed fairly are as follows:

- you're not capable of doing the job – perhaps due to not being sufficiently qualified, or poor performance
- due to your conduct – perhaps you've done something inappropriate or behaved poorly
- your role is no longer needed ('redundant')
- there is a legal reason why you cannot do your job – perhaps due to something with your immigration status, or, for example, if you are a delivery driver and have received a driving ban
- for 'some other substantial reason' – this covers various different situations, but it must still be a good reason

Remember that every situation is unique. If, for example, your employer has accepted the exact same behaviour from other colleagues but dismissed only you, or a fair procedure was not followed, you might still have a claim.

If you are dismissed for reasons to do with your conduct or your capability, you should read the 'Acas Code of Practice

on disciplinary and grievance procedures' and the 'disciplinary procedure step by step guide' on the Acas website (see
p. 277). These documents detail how your employer should
behave. For example, if poor performance is an issue, they
state that employers should try to resolve matters informally
first – perhaps by them having a conversation with you and
setting up a plan to help you improve.

If you are dismissed by your employer, you must be told
why, the date your contract will end, your notice period (more
on this shortly) and of your right to appeal the decision. If
you have worked for the employer for 2 years or more, you
have the right to ask for them to put in writing the reasons
for your dismissal. Your employer has 14 days to give this to
you. If you are pregnant or on maternity leave, the reasons
must also be put in writing – regardless of how long you have
worked for them. As will be explained later, if the reason for
the dismissal is *because* of your pregnancy or maternity leave,
this will automatically be unfair dismissal.

In terms of redundancy, your employer must follow a
consultation and selection process by law. The consultation
process will require your employer to have a genuine consultation with you before any redundancies are finalised, where,
among other things, your concerns can be discussed and your
employer can explain to you why changes are needed and
how employees will be selected for redundancy. The selection process must be fair and a selection criteria established
– for example, perhaps employees will receive scores based on

their work performance, attendance and disciplinary record, with those scoring lowest overall being the ones made redundant. There are a number of things you might be eligible for, including redundancy pay, time off from work to find a new job and a notice period.

Notice periods

Statutory notice is the minimum notice that your employer must give you by law. Contractual notice is the notice period stated in your contract – this may allow for a notice period longer than statutory notice, but it can never be less. If your contract states a notice period less than the statutory notice, you are well within your rights to assert that you want the statutory minimum.

Provided you are an **employee** and have worked for the employer for over a month, you will be entitled to statutory notice. How long the statutory notice period is will depend on how long you have worked for the employer. It is calculated as follows:

- over 1 month but under 2 years – statutory notice period is 1 week
- from 2 years to 12 years – statutory notice period is 1 week for every year worked
- 12 years and over – statutory notice period is 12 weeks

You will usually be entitled to be paid as normal while working through your notice period.

Some employment contracts mention something called 'payment in lieu of notice' (or PILON). This is where you leave the organisation straight away, but you get what you would have been paid had there been the notice period. Even if your employment contract does not mention payment in lieu of notice, this is something your employer may still choose to offer you.

Garden leave (it sounds more exciting than it is) is when you are told by your employer to not work for some or all of your notice period. This isn't due to your employer being generous, but often rather in an effort to protect their business interests. Let's say you work for a tech company and are put on notice. Your employer may, legitimately, think it's appropriate that you are off the premises for your notice period so that you cannot access confidential material that you could then take to a competitor. You are still an employee during any period of garden leave and must be paid as normal.

There are some occasions where the employer may be justified in dismissing you without giving you notice. Gross misconduct would be one such case – which could include, for example, getting into a physical fight at work or stealing something. In such a situation you will not be entitled to any notice and subsequently any notice pay. If there is work you have done that you have not yet been paid for, you are still entitled to such payment, along with any expenses you are owed, and holiday accrued.

Unfair dismissal

If you believe your dismissal was unfair, you will want to consider what your options are to challenge it. There are a few situations whereby if they amount to the main reason for you being dismissed, the dismissal is automatically classed as unfair.

Some examples of these are as follows:

- requesting something you are entitled to by law, such as being paid the minimum wage
- partaking in jury service
- being a member of a trade union
- being pregnant or on maternity leave
- taking action in relation to a health and safety issue, or proposing to do so
- whistleblowing (this is where you report your employer for wrongdoing: see p. 194)

You will usually have the right to make a claim to an employment tribunal for unfair dismissal if:

- you have employee status; and
- you have worked for your employer continuously for 2 years or more.

You have 3 months less 1 day from the date of the dismissal to make your claim. If your dismissal was for a reason that is automatically unfair (as discussed previously), there is no requirement that you have worked for your employer continuously for 2 years or more.

Be aware that even if your employer has a valid reason for dismissing you, their failure to follow a full and fair procedure may mean you have a case for unfair dismissal.

Constructive unfair dismissal

Feel like you've been pushed out of work by your employer? If your employer did something really serious that made you feel you had no choice but to leave the organisation, you might be able to claim for 'constructive unfair dismissal'. Examples might include being bullied or regularly not being paid what you are entitled to. If you are reading this and thinking of resigning due to the treatment you are receiving at work, it is worth seeking legal advice first, as constructive unfair dismissal claims are notoriously difficult to win. The difficulties can arise for many reasons, but will frequently be because the tribunal does not believe the behaviour was *so* serious that it entitled you to resign and treat yourself as dismissed, or perhaps believes you resigned as you wanted to start another job, as opposed to because of the treatment you were receiving. You will usually have the right to make a claim for constructive unfair dismissal if:

- you have employee status; and
- you have worked for your employer continuously for 2 years or more.

You have 3 months less 1 day to make your claim from when you resign. You must always inform Acas of your intention to make a claim, who will offer you 'early conciliation'. Early conciliation is where an impartial third party will see if an agreement can be reached between you and your employer without the need for things to go to an employment tribunal. More information on early conciliation can be found on Acas's website (see p. 277).

Wrongful dismissal

Wrongful dismissal occurs where your employer breaches the terms of your contract when dismissing you. It is often to do with notice or notice pay – so, for example, being dismissed without receiving a notice period or the notice pay you're entitled to.

If you were to be dismissed without notice for gross misconduct, but a tribunal later found that your actions did not actually amount to gross misconduct, you might be able to make a claim for wrongful dismissal.

You have 3 months less 1 day from the date of the dismissal to make your claim.

You do not need to have worked for your employer for a certain amount of time (i.e. 2 years) to be able to make a claim for wrongful dismissal.

Discriminatory dismissal

If you have been dismissed for a discriminatory reason, you can also make a claim based on your dismissal under the

Equality Act 2010. It does not matter how long you have been employed. You can make a claim to an employment tribunal provided your work comes under the broad definition of 'employment' in Section 83 of the Equality Act 2010 (note: this definition is broader than that which is provided in the 'Employment status' section at the start of this chapter – namely, it encompasses those who we would normally consider 'workers' and some self-employed persons).

I want to take action – where do I start?

If you want to appeal your dismissal, a useful starting point will be looking at your employer's appeal process. This should tell you the steps you need to take in order to appeal the dismissal. Your trade union, if you belong to one, may be able to help you. If you have tried this without success you may consider taking the next step – going to an employment tribunal. The Acas website (see p. 277) provides further information on this.

Whistleblowing

Having just got to grips with odd terms such as 'garden leave', it is time to tackle another: 'whistleblowing'. Whistleblowing is where you speak out against your employer's wrongdoing. Important to know here is that the thing you speak out about *must* be something that you reasonably believe to be in the public interest.

If you 'blow the whistle' in relation to any of the following, you will be protected by law:

- a criminal offence, such as fraud
- a breach of a legal obligation (for example your employer has the incorrect type of insurance)
- a miscarriage of justice
- somebody's health or safety being in danger
- a risk of environmental damage (or that environmental damage has occurred)
- information relating to any of the above that is being or is likely to be deliberately concealed

✓ The above bullet points serve as a quick overview. Read Section 43B(1) of the Employment Rights Act 1996 for more detail.

Being protected by law means that by blowing the whistle you should not suffer any detriment from your employer – for example, being treated unfairly or losing your job. If, however, you blow the whistle on activity that doesn't fit into the above criteria, you will not be protected by the whistle-blowing laws.

Your employer is generally the appropriate person to inform about your concern. If your employer has a whistle-blowing policy, this is worth reading in advance, as it should tell you how to blow the whistle (or make a 'protected disclosure' – the legal term) and what to expect. If you do not wish to report the concern to your employer, you can make the disclosure to a 'prescribed person' who is independent of your employer. A list of prescribed people and bodies can be found by googling 'whistleblowing list of prescribed people and bodies'. Click the gov.uk link.

It is not just employees who are protected by whistle-blowing laws, but also workers – e.g. agency staff.

Trade unions

A trade union is an organisation that looks after the interests of its members – usually employees or workers. Trade unions will often be involved in negotiations with employers in relation to pay, supporting members in disciplinary and grievance meetings, and discussing matters to do with redundancy or members' general concerns.

You have the legal right to join a union, or not to join a union. Your employer would be breaking the law if they were to threaten to subject you to unfair treatment if you do not leave a union, or if they were to offer you some form of 'benefit' to leave a trade union. They would also be breaking the law if they dismissed you because you were a union member (or were not), or if you took part or wanted to take part in union activities. You should also not be treated unfavourably by your employer for your union membership, or due to leaving a union, or due to you taking part in its meetings.

In the event that you feel that your employer has treated you unfairly due to your trade union membership (or lack of), you could consider raising a grievance or going to an employment tribunal.

Being self-employed

Having caught yourself a few too many times browsing 'what is it like to be self-employed' by the water dispenser in the office – you decide you're going to give it a go.

As somebody who is self-employed, you have very few employment rights, meaning this section is fairly short.

Two significant rights you *do* have are protection from discrimination (provided you have a contract to do work personally or you are a contract worker) and, while you are working on a client's premises, protection for your health and safety.

The majority of the rights you have will be those contained in the contract (oral or written) you have with the people/organisations you provide services to. As such, it is worth taking the time to make sure your contract is as robust as possible in order to protect you, and to have a written contract as opposed to an oral one. For example, let's say you are a freelancer – you may in your contract state a certain amount that will be charged for the late payment of fees.

When considering becoming self-employed, here are a few things you need to know:

Tax: When it comes to tax, you will be responsible for paying your own. Contact HMRC, who will be able to help set this up. You may wish to hire an accountant, particularly in the early days while you're still getting used to things, as you can receive penalties from HMRC if you make errors.

VAT: There are certain circumstances where you must pay VAT, and others where you may register voluntarily – which can have its benefits. Speaking to an accountant will help you choose what is right for you.

Insurance: You may legally be obliged to take out certain types of insurance depending on the business you are in and how you trade. Even where a type of insurance is not mandatory, you may feel it wise to take it out – for example, insurance on your stock.

What if I'm not paid for work I have done?

They say prevention is better than cure. You will find that some companies and individuals are awful at paying promptly, but something you can do to (hopefully) speed things up is have a clear invoicing process. Your accountant may be able to help with this, but if you don't have one, do some research on how you can make your invoicing process as seamless as possible. Clearly laid-out invoices make it easier for the accounts department at the company you're doing work for to quickly process your payment. If your invoice seems in any way confusing, they may put it on the back-burner and before you know it … days, months, years have elapsed …

If you have not been paid, in many instances a reminder should do the trick. This can be a gentle reminder (putting things in writing is nearly always the best option), or you may want to write a letter requesting your money. Chapter 12 may give you some inspiration on how to frame this letter, or on how to frame the formal conversation that may be required.

If the money is still proving hard to come by, depending on the circumstances, you may want to consider alternative dispute resolution (see p. 266).

As a last resort, legal action may be most appropriate. Chapter 12 deals with how to make a small claim.

✓ The stereotypical working from a coffee shop self-employed lifestyle has its perks, but one downside is that you can find yourself out of the loop when it comes to changes in your industry, as you are not in that office environment where people are continually talking. Consider joining professional communities related to your sector of work.

8

Alcohol and Other Drugs

The purpose of this book is to address real-life legal questions and offer tools for everyday situations. It is not here to judge; we are all human and we all have our vices, or do things we know we shouldn't – for some it may be excessive Netflix, for others it may be sweets for breakfast, and for some it may be a line of coke on a night out or a daily spliff. The key difference here is that Netflix and sweets are not illegal, while many recreational drugs are – hence their inclusion in this book.

For some people, drugs might be recreational. For others they can be an addiction. Because of their nature, what can often start as recreational can end up as an addiction, especially with the most addictive drugs (which include heroin, cocaine, alcohol and tobacco). One third of adults aged between 16 and 59 have taken an illegal drug at some point in their life. This chapter seeks to advise you of the reality of the legal situation so that, whatever choices you make, you are fully aware of the law.

The law on alcohol is also included in this chapter. While many of us know the basic rules, there's much more to the law around alcohol than just having to be 18 or over to buy it. This chapter aims to make it all clearer.

Whatever your association with drugs and alcohol, this chapter will serve you in helping to better understand its relationship to the law.

Alcohol

The UK is an 'alcocentric' society – although this is changing, with the proportion of the population who do not drink rising each year. Nonetheless, alcohol is widely accepted to the extent that it is still permissible to drink it at many professional events as well as, erm, extremely unprofessional events. But whether you're drinking a glass of the priciest Bordeaux with business clients, or just a tinny in the garden with your mates, certain rules apply.

Buying alcohol for under 18s

It is illegal for somebody under 18 to buy alcohol, or attempt to buy it, and it is illegal for a person to sell alcohol to somebody under 18. If you are 18 or over and buy or attempt to buy alcohol for somebody under 18, you break the law.

If somebody under 18 is in a licensed premises, say a pub or restaurant, it is illegal for them to drink alcohol. The exception to this is if they are aged 16 or 17 and accompanied by an adult – in which case they can drink (but not buy) cider, beer or wine with a meal. If a person is 16 or 17 and works in a restaurant, they can serve alcohol as long as the licence-holder or bar manager approves the sale.

If somebody under 18 is drinking in public, say in the local park, the police can confiscate the alcohol. If caught three times, the police could potentially arrest the person.

If somebody is under 18 and they attempt to use a 'fake ID' (perhaps an older brother's ID, or their own but with the date of birth altered) to, for example, purchase alcohol at a shop or enter an adult venue such as a nightclub, depending on the circumstances they may commit offences under the Identity Documents Act 2010, Forgery and Counterfeiting Act 1981 and/or Fraud Act 2006. If they are caught, the ID is likely to be seized and they may be reported to the police. There are a number of options as to what may happen next – for example, the police may take steps to educate the individual on the risks and consequences of using a fake ID.

✓ The law does not prohibit a child aged 5 to 16 from drinking at home or other private premises. Nonetheless, Chief Medical Officers' guidance states that an alcohol-free childhood is advisable.

The law on alcohol for those 18 or over

Drinking alcohol in public

Many people wonder if they can drink alcohol on the street – we've all seen the sneaky beer in a brown paper bag. The answer is yes. You can drink alcohol in public as long as you are 18 or over. There are some areas where this may not be allowed though – for example where a Public Space Protection Order (PSPO) is in place. A PSPO enables a police officer to stop you drinking in that area and to confiscate your alcohol.

Similar to drinking in public, there is a little confusion over the law on drinking on trains. National trains in the UK sell alcohol which you can buy and drink. You can also drink alcohol you have brought onto the train. Nonetheless, some train operators will run 'dry' trains where you are unable to have or consume alcohol on board. This is sometimes done for trains transporting people to large sporting events, for example football matches.

For those that travel on the Tube in London, although the Central Line on a Saturday night might suggest otherwise, Transport for London has a ban on passengers drinking on board all their services, which includes buses, trams, the Overground and the Tube.

Being drunk

Selling alcohol to a drunk person

It is illegal to knowingly *sell* alcohol, or *attempt* to sell alcohol, or *allow* alcohol to be sold to, a person who is drunk. The maximum fine for the person who sells the alcohol to someone who is drunk is £1,000 and the licence-holder of the pub, bar, restaurant, corner shop or supermarket can lose their licence completely if they are found to have sold alcohol to someone who is drunk, or allowed it to happen. Unfortunately, there is little guidance about what constitutes a drunk person.

Is being drunk illegal?

Being drunk is not illegal. Nonetheless, if you are disorderly too – perhaps shouting or threatening someone – you may commit offences such as being drunk and disorderly.

Being intoxicated and criminal offending

This short section will explore the law where a person's excuse for an offence is words to the effect of: 'I only did it because I was drunk!'

Use of the word 'intoxication' in this context refers to being intoxicated through drink or drugs.

The general rule is that intoxication is not a defence. It can, however, be a little less straightforward when the level of intoxication is *so* significant that you are unable to form the necessary '*mens rea*' for the crime. *Mens rea* is a Latin term and translates as 'guilty mind'. For many crimes, in order to be found guilty, both the physical and the mental element of the crime need to be present. You need to not only have done the guilty act (the physical element), but also had a guilty mind too (the mental element) – in other words, you intended to do the guilty act (or were reckless as to it being done).

For more information, google 'intoxication legal guidance' and click the Crown Prosecution Service (CPS) link.

The webpage is comprehensive and contains a wide variety of interesting information – for example, the fact that if you deliberately make yourself intoxicated in order to give yourself the courage to commit an offence, you cannot use the fact that you were intoxicated as a defence.

Alcohol and driving

You already know you shouldn't drink and drive. But let's get specific. The drink driving limit is as follows:

- 35 micrograms of alcohol per 100 millilitres of breath
- 80 milligrams of alcohol per 100 millilitres of blood
- 107 milligrams of alcohol per 100 millilitres of urine

These quantities can't easily be converted into a certain number of units of alcohol, or types of drinks, because factors such as how fast your body absorbs alcohol, your sex and your body mass will all have an impact on how much alcohol you have in your bloodstream. While there is a lot of 'rule of thumb' guidance on the internet as to how much you can drink, I won't include it here for the simple fact that, from my experience as a lawyer, the only foolproof way to be sure is to not have any alcohol in your system when driving.

✓If you've been drinking the night before, it is important to remember that you may still be over the legal limit if you drive the next day.

Drink driving penalties

So, let's say you are driving (or attempting to drive) a vehicle, are breathalysed, and subsequently are found to be over the legal alcohol limit. What are the consequences? It depends on a number of factors, such as how far over the legal limit you are, and whether it is your first offence.

You could receive:

- up to 6 months in prison
- an unlimited fine
- a driving ban for at least 1 year

Controlled drug classes and maximum punishments for possession

Illegal drugs can be differentiated by their class. The drug classes are determined by Parliament, and they are intended to indicate how dangerous certain drugs are, as well as the severity of punishment associated with them. Class A drugs are considered the most harmful, and possession of them carries the harshest punishment.

While this chapter focuses on possession and not supply, I've included a line on the penalties for supply too. Remember: supply does not only refer to large-scale industrial operations, but potentially if you are 'just' selling to your friends (or even 'just' giving to friends – supply does not require that you make a profit). The sentence you receive will depend, among other things, on the quantity of the drug concerned. I have listed examples of drugs falling into the different class categories below. It is worth noting that some of these drugs are pharmaceutical drugs. This chapter assumes you are in possession of the drug in a context other than you having the authorisation to have it – such as a prescription.

The legal penalty for possession of the different classes is as follows:

Class A: Possession carries up to 7 years in prison, an unlimited fine, or both. Supplying holds a maximum sentence of life in prison, an unlimited fine, or both.

Class A drugs include: cocaine; ecstasy (MDMA); heroin; LSD; and magic mushrooms.

Class B: Possession carries up to 5 years in prison, an unlimited fine, or both. Supplying holds a maximum sentence of 14 years in prison, an unlimited fine, or both.

Class B drugs include: cannabis; codeine; ketamine; mephedrone; speed; and synthetic cannabinoids (e.g. Spice).

Class C: Possession carries up to 2 years in prison, an unlimited fine, or both (however, it is not illegal to possess anabolic steroids for personal use). Supplying holds a maximum sentence of 14 years in prison, an unlimited fine, or both.

Class C drugs include: anabolic steroids; and piperazines (similar to ecstasy pills). Benzodiazepines are Class C drugs, but many are also available on prescription (more on this shortly).

It is worth adding that, as per the sentencing guidelines used in courts to determine the punishment an individual will receive for being caught in the possession of a drug, you won't get a maximum sentence (or anything remotely close to it), save for in the most serious of cases. Nonetheless, the descriptions earlier give a sense of how the court *has the power* to act. See the section on the next page for a better sense of how you are likely to be treated if you are found in possession of a small quantity of a drug for personal use.

✓ Diazepam (Valium), alprazolam (Xanax) and codeine are examples of drugs intended for prescription use that have found their way onto the street. These can be lawfully possessed only with a prescription. Without one, Valium and Xanax are categorised as Class C drugs, and codeine as Class B. Recent years have seen a rise in 'street-benzos', which are, in effect, fake versions of prescription benzodiazepines packaged to look as if they are genuine. 'Street-benzos' are Class C drugs.

Can I be arrested for having consumed a substance (e.g. smoked a joint), but none is now left?

No – use of the drug is not an offence, whereas possession is. Nonetheless, if taking the drug has affected your behaviour and, for example, made you act aggressively towards others – you could be arrested for offences in relation to that.

Also remember that *drug* driving is a thing – not just *drink* driving. If you drive under the influence of drugs you can receive a large fine, be banned from driving and could even go to prison.

✓ If you are in control of a premises such as a nightclub or bar, there is the potential for you to be prosecuted if you knowingly permit or tolerate drug dealing or the smoking of cannabis at the premises. See Section 8 of the Misuse of Drugs Act 1971 for more information.

What happens if I'm caught in possession of a drug?

A framework for police forces to implement the use of 'Out of Court Disposals' was issued in 2017 by the National Police Chiefs' Council. The full 44-page document can be found by googling 'charging and out of court disposals – a national strategy'. The term 'Out of Court Disposal' refers to a range of options open to the police that can be used as alternatives to prosecution, enabling them to deal with low-level offending in a proportionate manner. The framework envisages three main potential responses when a person is found in possession of a drug for personal use, which I will set out. Nonetheless, it is important to note that there may be variation among how different police forces deal with matters, and the information that follows is in no way intended to be a complete guide, or to state all of the options in terms of how such matters will be dealt with.

Community resolution

If it's your first time being found in possession of a controlled drug (or potentially if it is not the first occasion, but more than 12 months have elapsed since the previous occasion), you can be offered a community resolution. These can be given on the street (i.e. without being arrested and taken to a police station). While a community resolution does not count as a criminal conviction and will not form part of your criminal record, it *may* be disclosable in an enhanced Disclosure and Barring Service (DBS) check, but won't be as a matter of routine. The disclosure will be on the basis it is relevant to the job applied for (see p. 275 for more information).

In order to be eligible to receive a community resolution, you must admit responsibility (which, in effect, is an admission of possession).

The community resolution will have conditions as part of it – for example, you may have to participate in an educational course about drugs. Failure to comply with the conditions of a community resolution puts you at risk of prosecution.

Conditional caution

You may receive a conditional caution if it is not thought that a community resolution is appropriate, or you have already recently received a community resolution. A conditional caution is less severe than a conviction but *does* form part of your criminal record.

In order to be eligible for a conditional caution, the prospect of you being convicted for the offence were you to be charged must be 'realistic', and you must also admit guilt of the offence. Before admitting guilt to a conditional caution, it can be a good idea to seek legal advice.

Conditions that may be attached to the conditional caution include attending an educational course and undertaking unpaid work. Failure to comply with the conditions can lead to you being prosecuted for the original offence (i.e. the possession of the drug).

As per the framework, only in exceptional circumstances would a person receive a second conditional caution – an example being if over 2 years have passed since the issuing of the earlier conditional caution.

Charge

You may be charged if the police don't consider the options discussed above as being appropriate, or because you have already received a conditional caution. Being charged will result in you receiving something called a 'summons' (usually sent in the post). This will tell you what you have been charged with and when you are required to attend a hearing at the magistrates' court.

✓ If you are under 18 and caught in possession of a drug, the police can inform your parent, guardian or carer.

✓ Possession includes being 'in control' of a substance. In other words, it does not need to be physically on you. If the substance is, say, in a rucksack in your bedroom, and you are elsewhere – you could still be found guilty of the offence.

Other drugs

Sexual offences and drugs

The effects of two Class C drugs require particular attention due to the frequency at which they are used in the context of sexual offences. These are Rohypnol (a form of benzodiazepine) and GHB/GBL.

Rohypnol commonly looks like a tablet/pill. When people talk about drinks being spiked in nightclubs, this is often the drug they are referring to – the pill dissolves in the drink.

GHB and GBL look the same as each other. They will commonly appear as a colourless and oily liquid. They can also, but more rarely, appear in capsule or powder/paste form.

These drugs can impair a person's memory and make them physically less able to defend themselves.

It is an offence under Section 61 of the Sexual Offences Act 2003 if, without consent, a person gives another person a substance with the intention of overpowering them so that they can engage in sexual activity. This carries a punishment of up to 10 years in prison.

✓ In 2021, the Home Office indicated that GHB/GBL would be moving from a Class C to a Class B drug. At the time of writing, this change has not taken place.

✓ Alcohol is probably the most common substance used in order to overpower someone for the purposes of engaging in sexual activity. Section 61 of the Sexual Offences Act 2003 would cover situations where an individual's drink is spiked and therefore they did not know they were consuming alcohol. It would not, however, cover a situation where someone encourages an individual to get drunk so that they can engage in sexual activity with them, where the individual knew they were consuming alcohol.

Psychoactive substances

The Psychoactive Substances Act 2016 amended the previously held position on many 'legal highs'. A substance deserving particular attention is nitrous oxide (otherwise known as 'laughing gas' or 'nos', among others). Nitrous oxide is the name of a gas, found in the metal canisters you often see lining town-centre streets early on a Sunday morning once revellers from the night before have gone home. While possession is not illegal, supplying it (where the supplier knows or is reckless as to whether it is likely to be consumed by others) carries a maximum sentence of 7 years in prison, an unlimited fine, or both.

9

The Digital World

Alexa wakes me up, Alexa reminds me to take my cooking out of the oven, and on a daily basis – with remarkable accuracy I might add – Alexa confirms that it will be raining today in Manchester.

Clearly, the digital world is no longer something separate from our 'real world', but is deeply embedded in it. Research shows people on average now spend the equivalent of a full day (24 hours) per week online. Whether it's through our smart devices, our computers or our phones, it's getting harder to see the distinction between online and IRL.

In the same way that knowing your rights in the 'real world' is crucial, knowing your rights in the digital world is too.

We'll be looking at our rights when it comes to our devices, accounts, and what we say and do online. So, although on some occasions we may feel it insignificant when we impulsively post to our social media accounts (for example, Instagramming last night's meal at a restaurant), there are occasions where what we post can have serious legal consequences.

This chapter won't just consider the things being broadcast from your smartphone or laptop, but also what is contained within them. Our smartphones house some of the most private information about us. While you might see it as a no-brainer that your mates can't have the PIN to your phone, you ought to know the laws that exist when an authority, such as the police, requests such information. There are times when you can refuse, and times it might require a bit more thought.

Laws all social media users should know

'Think before you tweet,' a wise person once told me. If you've got a social media account, you should become acquainted with the laws covered in this section. Not only can a misjudged tweet (or Facebook post, Instagram caption or TikTok video) cause reputational damage, it can also land you in trouble with the law.

Defamation

'Defamation' is a word we have all come across – but one we often associate with the rich and famous. Nonetheless, it can have wider applicability too.

Defamation refers to the publication of a statement that tends to lower the claimant (i.e. the 'victim') in the estimation of right-thinking members of society generally. A statement will not be deemed as defamatory unless its publication has caused or is likely to cause serious harm to the claimant's reputation.

Defamation can be one of two things: libel, or slander. So what's the difference?

Libel generally relates to publications that have an element of permanence in nature – so, for example, things written in a book or newspaper, or even things said on the radio or TV. Even though 'permanence' may sound more like something chiselled into rock, a tweet that took you five seconds to compose could amount to libel. So could a retweet.

Slander generally relates to publications that are more fleeting in their nature. They don't tend to have the same 'permanence' as libel. Spoken words between two individuals may amount to slander; even physical gestures might.

What about if somebody has accused you of publishing a defamatory statement? What are your defences?

If you have been accused of publishing a defamatory statement, there are four main defences that I anticipate the typical reader of this book may be able to draw on.

1. **Truth.** Someone might not like what you post, but if it is true, then it is not defamatory.
2. **Honest opinion.** This will be a defence if you can show that what you published was your honest opinion, that the basis of the opinion was indicated, and that an honest

person could have held that opinion based on any fact that existed at the time the statement was made. Reliance on untrue statements of fact made by others will not suffice.

3. The publication is a matter of **public interest**. In other words, publishing the statement was in the public interest when considering all the circumstances and you reasonably believed that publishing it was in the public interest. This defence is often used by news publishers who are writing about public figures on matters that are in the public interest, even if it may be reputationally damaging, such as corruption or inappropriate behaviour.

4. Some communications are considered **privileged** in defamation law, which protects the person making the communication from being sued. This is because of public policy reasons (or put simply, to ensure that people are able to speak freely on matters that are important for the functioning of society).

There are two types of privilege – **absolute** and **qualified**.

Absolute privilege is a complete defence. It applies, for example, to statements made in court.

There are two types of qualified privilege: **statutory qualified privilege** and **common law qualified privilege**.

- Statutory qualified privilege attaches to specific things detailed in the Defamation Act 2013, such as a fair and accurate report of parliamentary proceedings. None-theless, this defence will be defeated if the claimant can show that the defendant acted maliciously in publishing the statement. (Note: although the defamatory nature of the publication may seem sufficient to show malice, other evidence will usually be needed.)

- Common law qualified privilege provides a person with a defence if they made the statement in circumstances where they had a legal, social or moral duty or interest to do so, and the person to whom the statement was made had a corresponding interest in receiving it; for example, the providing of an employment reference or a person reporting a crime to the police.

What are your options if you feel that you have been victim of libel or slander?

Depending on the nature of the publication and where it is being communicated, you may first want to see if the material can be removed using the takedown procedures on a plat-form. So, for example, if the offending publication breaches the platform's community standards or terms of use, this may be a way to get it removed. To find this information, google '[name of platform – e.g. 'facebook'] 'community standards' / 'terms of service' / 'user agreement'.

You can also send a complaint letter – telling the person/platform to remove the post/publication and not make any further comments of a similar nature. See p. 260 for general suggestions on how you can go about writing a complaint letter. Particularly if the matter is serious, you may wish to consider obtaining legal advice.

Another option is to make a 'right to be forgotten' request to Google (or indeed any search engine) – which can result in them delisting the URL. This means that the URL won't show up in Google's search results. While this will make the URL harder to find (it won't show up on a Google search), it won't remove the publication entirely. A right to be forgotten request is therefore not always a solution (see p. 225 for more information).

Of course, while these options are being pursued it is important to keep in mind the 1-year limitation on a defamation claim. This means you have 1 year from the date of publication to make your claim.

✓Even if you want to take legal action, making a defamation claim might not always be the best option. They are often very expensive. Other options you may wish to consider include making a claim for harassment, and making a claim for a personal data breach and/or for misuse of private information. A lawyer working in these areas will be able to assist further. You might also be able to obtain advice from the Information Commissioner's Office (see p. 280).

Online bullying

On most social media platforms, measures are in place enabling you to block an account so that the owner of it cannot communicate with you. If the social media platform allows you to report the account, this might also be a good idea, as it may help protect somebody else.

There have been successful cases of people taking legal action against their trolls. If taking legal action is something you are even remotely considering, remember to keep all messages as evidence – screenshot them if need be. This will help strengthen your case.

How private is your digital life?

Try to grab someone's phone and the speed at which they will grab it back from you is remarkable. It's not that there's anything illegal on it, but our phones house some of our most private information and, as such, are something that we are very protective of. But how private are we actually being when we're online? Who are we inadvertently letting in, and what are our rights when it comes to who can see what is in our digital lives?

Devices

Most devices nowadays are password protected. This makes it pretty easy to prevent access to anyone who might want to look inside.

A situation that might be more complicated is if it's the police who are asking. The police can ask for your PIN, just as anybody else might. You can certainly give it to them. If for whatever reason, however, you do not want to, then you are absolutely within your rights to say no.

If you refuse, but the police still want access to your phone, they may rely on Section 49 of the Regulation of Investigatory Powers Act 2000. In such a situation, police can give you a notice (known as a Section 49 notice) stating that they require you to provide the PIN or encryption key to allow them access to your device. The police cannot give this notice off their own back; they must obtain written permission from a circuit judge or a district judge. With this, they acquire the appropriate permission to make the request for your PIN or encryption key.

Whereas before you were perfectly within your rights to refuse to give them access, now, failing to comply with the notice would be a criminal offence with a maximum prison sentence of 2 years (or a maximum of 5 years in certain situations).

If you genuinely don't know your PIN, you can put this forward as a defence.

✓ Beware of official-looking documents from the police that suggest giving your PIN is compulsory. Obtaining your PIN is a big deal. If the police have not received authorisation from the court, you do not need to provide your PIN.

✓ If a case goes to trial and, although you were not given a Section 49 notice, you refused to hand over your PIN, the prosecution may use this fact to say that you 'clearly had something to hide'.

Accounts

You can make decisions about how your accounts will be dealt with when you die. At the time of writing, the policies for some of the biggest social media companies are as follows:

Facebook allows you to opt for your account to be permanently deleted when you die. You can also opt for your account to be 'memorialised', which means it will be visible to others but with the word 'Remembering' in front of your name. Once an account is memorialised, it cannot be logged in to – meaning it cannot be hacked. Facebook can learn of your death by somebody (such as a friend) filling out a form stating that you have passed away, along with proof. Alternatively, you can appoint a 'legacy contact' in advance of your death. Among a few other things, this person can update your profile photo and manage the tributes that people share on your account. They cannot read your messages (or log in to your account more generally). You can make decisions about what happens to your Facebook account when you die through the settings menu.

Twitter's policy states that they will work with an individual who is authorised to act on behalf of your estate or with a 'verified immediate family member of the deceased' to have an account deactivated. Such a person will have to fill in a form and send it to Twitter in order to get this in motion. The approach taken by **LinkedIn** is similar; however, it does not appear that the person filling in the form needs to have had such a close relationship with you – they could have been, for example, a colleague.

Instagram requires an individual to fill in a form for your account to be memorialised. They will require proof of death, such as a news article or link to an obituary. If the account is memorialised, nobody else will be able to log in to it – preventing it from being hacked. Verified family members can also get in touch with Instagram to request that your account be deleted.

Internet cookies

Every time you use the internet, you leave traces …

By now, all readers who use the internet regularly will be familiar with the term 'cookies'. When visiting a website, you will very often be met with a message to the effect of: '[Name of website] uses cookies to ensure you get the best experience on our website', before providing you with an option to 'accept cookies', or perhaps 'reject cookies', or 'more options'. Many of us will accept, or reject, but with little knowledge as to why – maybe you click whichever button is closest to the mouse cursor. The next few paragraphs seek to provide some clarity.

The first time you visit a website, you will be asked to accept cookies. If you decline, depending on the website, you may experience limited functionality or a diminished user experience. If you accept these cookies, you essentially accept a tag with a unique identifier that will be stored on your device. Every time you go back to that specific website, as a result of this tag, the website knows that the person viewing the website is you. This might mean that, for example, when clicking back onto a website, the shopping basket full of items you had previously selected is still there.

Cookies are stored on *your* device. This means you are able to delete them if you so wish. The way to do this is usually via the settings of your web browser, close to the options to view your search history or bookmark a webpage.

There are different types of cookies, but for the purposes of this chapter we will focus on the most common ones – first-party and third-party cookies.

First-party cookies relate to those that are linked to the specific website that you are visiting. These will have various purposes but may include improving customer experience – for example, remembering your language preferences.

Third-party cookies refer to those stored on your device that do not necessarily belong to the website you are browsing but rather a third-party company (or companies). An example might be the 'live chat' function on a website. Sometimes these live chat functions will say 'live chat – powered by [third-party company name]'. Such a scenario would typically indicate that there are third-party cookies present on the website you are browsing.

Additionally, some third-party cookies are able to track your activity on different websites and display targeted ads. This is why, having been on a retail website pondering the purchase of a pair of jeans, you may then be surprised to find the exact same pair of jeans, or a similar pair, appearing in an ad when browsing elsewhere on the internet. You have been the recipient of a targeted ad by virtue of third-party cookies.

Cookies (and third-party cookies more specifically) have caused unease among many privacy advocates who have concerns surrounding data ethics, the potential invasion of privacy and a potential lack of transparency. The lack of transparency has been somewhat addressed in legislation requiring websites to:

1. tell users the cookies are present on a website;
2. explain what the cookies are doing and why; and
3. get the person's consent to store cookies on their device.

Companies must also have a cookies policy/notice which explains the type of cookies used (first- or third-party) on their website, their purpose(s) and how the cookies can be managed.

UK GDPR: The right to be forgotten

In a deep dark corner of the internet, I am sure lies a social media account I made when I was 12 displaying a particularly questionable dress sense. As is the way with the internet, it might linger on forever, to be discovered and derided by my grandchildren (or just future colleagues). Anyone who grew up on the internet, or has spent any significant amount of time there, will have such records of their past selves, along with hundreds of dead accounts on shopping sites, old addresses and random bits of personal information. But what if you don't want to be remembered as the kid with the trilby? What if you don't want to be remembered online at all?

The right to be forgotten is more formally known as the 'right to erasure'. Under Article 17 of UK GDPR (General Data Protection Regulation), in certain circumstances, you can ask for data that an organisation holds about you to be erased.

Examples include:

- If the original reason the organisation needed your data no longer exists. For example, if you cancel your membership at the library, there is no longer a need for them to keep a record of your name and address.
- You were a child and the data was collected from you for an online service – for example, if you made a social media account as a 15-year-old. By virtue of this information having been collected from you as a child, you have the right to have it erased now, even as an adult.
- Your data was collected or used unlawfully by the organisation. For example, they did not comply with data protection rules.
- You have withdrawn your consent, having initially consented to use of your data by the organisation. For example, if you opted in for a survey but have since changed your mind.

You can make a request verbally or in writing for your information to be erased. The organisation will have to respond to your request within 1 month (however, they can request an extra 2 months depending on the complexity of the request). It is not an absolute right and the organisation may be able to refuse depending on the circumstances.

10

Activism

We live in a time when big issues dominate our lives: injustices and outrages fill the news, and something terrible that happens on one side of the world is known about within minutes on the other. It can feel like so much needs to change.

Within our lifetimes, experts predict that the effects of climate change will be irreversible unless we make radical changes. Social media has allowed people the world over to witness the death of a Black man at the hands of the police. Women are still warned not to walk home alone; in the space of 10 years, university fees tripled; and 30 per cent of children in the UK now live in poverty, while thousands of families rely on foodbanks. We may feel overwhelmed by the bad, but we also live in a time where global movements are built overnight, where one teenager's school strike can inspire millions around the world, and where there exist many spaces for protesting and voicing our dissent.

Activism can take many forms, whether that be writing

letters to your MP or being vocal on social media, signing petitions or taking to the streets with banners. Frustration with more passive forms of activism can mount: one too many auto-replies from your MP stating 'We hope to reply to your query within 2 weeks ...' can make even the most patient of us think, 'the system is a joke'.

Seldom does power cede easily, and this chapter is all about activism – your right to protest, your rights even when challenging powerful institutions, and how the law fits into it all.

Your right to protest

There comes a time in most people's lives when there is an urgent need to jump off the sofa after watching the news or listening to the radio and say, 'we need to do something!' – whether it be about climate change, animal rights or racial equality. You are tired of shouting at the TV and decide that you need to be out there protesting. From the suffragette movement in the early twentieth century, to the Gay Liberation Front protests, from the anti-war rallies of the 1960s and 2000s to the NUS student fees marches, the UK has a long history of protest. Protesting is by its very nature often disruptive, and, as such, carries risks for the individuals partaking in it. Nonetheless, it can help raise awareness of extremely important issues. This next section will tell you all about the things you ought to have an understanding of.

Fundamental legal rights

Our right to freedom of expression is protected by Article 10 of the European Convention on Human Rights, incorporated into UK law through the Human Rights Act 1998. We have the right to freely share our opinions without the state interfering. This might be through writing articles or posts on social media, or aloud, at a protest.

Article 11 of the European Convention on Human Rights, incorporated into UK law through the Human Rights Act 1998, protects your right to freedom of peaceful assembly and association. It gives you the right to demonstrate and march in a public space – even if others don't agree with your reasons.

However, these rights are not absolute and the state can restrict them so long as the restriction is prescribed by law, necessary, and proportionate. The restriction could be to protect public safety, or perhaps to protect the rights of other people. Nonetheless, the need for any such restriction to be proportionate means that it must not do more than is necessary to address the issue. In other words, the state cannot use a sledgehammer to crack a nut. The police, as a public authority, should take all reasonable steps to facilitate peaceful protest, as opposed to stopping it.

Organising a protest

If you are organising a protest, the first thing you will want to think about is whether you want your protest to be a public procession or a public assembly.

Public processions are when people will be moving along a route – think of a march.

Public assemblies are when people are gathered in a location – think of a group with placards outside a local leisure centre, protesting over its impending closure.

Organising a public procession

1) **Notice:** The first thing to note is that the law requires you to deliver written notice to the police at least 6 days before the proposed start date of the procession.

Your written notice must detail: the date and time of the procession, the proposed route, and the names and addresses of the organisers.

This written notice is to be given to a police station local to the area in which the procession will be starting.

✓ The law states that if giving at least 6 days' notice would not be reasonably practicable, you must inform the police as soon as you can. It is worth knowing that the police cannot stop a procession solely because notice was not given.

2) **Conditions:** The next thing to be aware of are the conditions that can be imposed on your protest. Being mindful of these early on can help you consider in your planning how you may be able to avoid them. For both a public procession and a public assembly, conditions can be imposed on the protest by a senior police officer if they believe that either:

- it may result in serious public disorder, serious damage

to property or serious disruption to the life of the community, or
- the reason you are organising it is to intimidate others into not doing something they have a right to do, or into doing something that they have a right not to do.

The conditions that could be imposed include, but are not limited to, restricting the route of the protest or prohibiting the protest from entering a certain public place.

3) **Prohibition:** A public procession can be banned at any time if the chief officer of police reasonably believes that, because of particular circumstances existing in a particular area, the power to impose conditions will not be sufficient to prevent the holding of public processions in that area from resulting in serious public disorder.

Organising a public assembly

1) **Notice:** Unlike a public procession, there is no legal requirement that you give the police advance notice. Many organisers of public assemblies make the tactical decision not to inform the police as they do not want to encourage them to impose conditions on the protest. Not telling the police of your intention to protest does not prevent them from imposing restrictions or requirements on the protest when they do learn about it. They could impose restrictions or requirements before it starts, or while it is in progress.

2) **Conditions:** Conditions can be imposed on the assembly by a senior police officer for the same reasons that apply to a procession. However, there is a limit to the conditions that can be imposed. There can only be conditions as to the place at which the assembly may be held (or continue to be held), its maximum duration, and the maximum number of persons who may constitute the assembly.

3) **Prohibition:** If an assembly of 20 or more people is to be held, it can be banned if the chief officer of police reasonably believes that it is intended to be held in any place on outside land to which the public has no right of access (or only a limited right of access – for example where the public can only be there for a particular purpose); and

- the assembly is likely to be held without the permission of the occupier of the land or is likely to conduct itself in such a way as to exceed the limits of the occupier's permission or the public's right of access; and
- the assembly may result in serious disruption to the life of the community or
- significant damage to the land, or a building or a monument which is of historical, architectural, archaeological or scientific importance.

✓ There has been considerable mention above of the conditions that a 'senior police officer' can put on a protest. You may be wondering who amounts to a senior police officer. If a procession is being held, or people are assembling with a view to taking part in it (think people walking towards it with their faces painted ready to take part), the senior police officer is the most senior in rank of the police officers present at the scene. In relation to a procession intended to be held (for example when the police become aware of your intention for the public procession but it is yet to take place), the conditions must be stated in writing from the chief officer of police.

Going to a protest

While carrying your placards and face paint, ensure that you too are carrying a working knowledge of what the law says in a variety of situations you may find yourself in.

Can the police take a photo of me?

If you are arrested, detained by a PCSO (police community support officer), given a dispersal direction (see p. 237) or given a fixed penalty notice, the police have the specific power to take photographs of you. They do not need your consent and, if necessary, can use reasonable force. However, you must be told the purpose and grounds for the photograph being taken and the purposes for which it may be used, disclosed or retained. The police can require you to remove items or substances covering your head or face in order to take this photograph. Examples might be a scarf, bandana, or face paint.

If you are not in one of the above categories and a photo is being taken of you, there is absolutely nothing wrong with covering your face so that you cannot be identified.

Can I take a photo of an officer?

Yes. In fact, the Metropolitan Police on their website state as follows: 'Members of the public and the media do not need a permit to film or photograph in public places and police have no power to stop them filming or photographing incidents of police personnel.' This applies to all forces, not just the Met.

Despite this clear statement, you should be aware that the police *could* stop and search you for filming or taking photographs if they reasonably suspect you to be a terrorist. The search would be for the limited purpose of discovering whether you have in your possession anything which may constitute evidence that you are a terrorist.

On their website, the Metropolitan Police state: 'Officers do not have the power to delete digital images or destroy film at any point during a search.'

Do I have to answer questions from the police?

No. See the stop and account section on p. 248. You do not have to tell them your name, what you are doing or where you are going (or even respond at all). Beware, however: giving false information could put you at risk of arrest for obstructing an officer in the execution of their duty.

Can the police make me remove my face covering?

Not unless a Section 60 authorisation is in force or a Section 60AA authorisation has been given. In such circumstances, the police have the power to require the removal of 'disguises'.

See p. 253 for more information on this. The police must make efforts to advise the public when a Section 60 authorisation is in force – regularly checking the Twitter account of the police force local to the protest to see if mention has been made of Section 60 is a good idea. You can ask the police, too. See also 'Can the police take a photo of me?' earlier.

Can the police stop and search me?

The police's stop and search powers are the same at a protest as they are anywhere else. See p. 248, and 'Can I take a photo of an officer?'.

What do I need to know if I find myself in a kettle?

Kettling is a police tactic frequently used in protests whereby the police will surround protesters in order to keep them in one particular place. A kettle can be imposed where the police deem it necessary to prevent a breach of the peace, serious injury or damage. It should not be imposed for any longer than necessary and certainly should not be used where there are less intrusive ways for the police to prevent the breach of the peace, serious injury or damage. Recent years have seen a notable increase in the use of kettling and also their duration, frequently lasting for several hours. Because of how distressing and frustrating it can be to find yourself in a kettle, it can be tempting to do anything at all to get out of it. It is therefore important to know that the police cannot require you to give your personal details or be photographed (see 'Can the police take a photo of me?') as a trade-off for being allowed to leave the kettle. It is also important to know that the police do not have any particular special powers to stop and search in a kettle – the exact same rules apply for stop and search whether you are in a kettle or outside of one.

✓ It is always worth keeping charge on your phone during a kettle. While the temptation might be to use your phone as a means of quelling your boredom, if the kettle lasts for a number of hours, you may need to rely on your phone to plan alternative transport back home, inform loved ones of your whereabouts, or to record an incident that concerns you.

✓ If going to a protest, take water and something to eat with you. More than you think you need. You may well be unable to leave the protest when you intend to due to police cordons or kettling.

Ways a protest can be stopped

If you are organising a protest, you should be aware of both the police's power to make a dispersal direction under Section 35 of the Anti-social Behaviour, Crime and Policing Act 2014 and a local authority's power to make a Public Space Protection Order (PSPO). These are two ways organisers can be caught off guard and a protest be prohibited. Both pieces of legislation should be read in full; however, an overview is provided below.

Dispersal direction

An officer of at least the rank of inspector can implement

dispersal powers if they are satisfied on reasonable grounds that dispersal is necessary in order to remove or reduce the likelihood of:

1. members of the public in the locality being harassed, alarmed or distressed; or
2. the occurrence in the locality of crime and disorder.

Dispersal powers can have effect for up to 48 hours.

This will then enable a constable in uniform or community support officer to direct a person to leave the locality (or part of it) and not return for a specified period (up to 48 hours), provided that they have reasonable grounds to suspect that the behaviour of that person has contributed to or is likely to contribute to the matters described above.

If you are planning on organising a protest, more information about this can be found in Section 35 of the Anti-social Behaviour, Crime and Policing Act 2014.

Public Space Protection Order (PSPO)

In brief, under Section 59 of the Anti-social Behaviour, Crime and Policing Act 2014, a PSPO can prohibit certain activities taking place in a certain area, and/or impose requirements upon people who are carrying out certain activities in that area.

A local authority may make such an order if satisfied on reasonable grounds that two conditions are met.

Condition 1

1. activities carried out in a public place within the authority's area have had a detrimental effect on the quality of life of those in the locality; **or**
2. it is likely that activities will be carried on in a public place within that area and that they will have such an effect;

   AND the effect, or likely effect, of the activities

Condition 2

1. is, or is likely to be, of a persistent or continuing nature;
2. is, or is likely to be, such as to make the activities unreasonable; and
3. justifies the restrictions imposed by the notice.

You can find more about this in Section 59 of the Antisocial Behaviour, Crime and Policing Act 2014.

Police should give you the chance to leave the area voluntarily. If you do not do so, you can receive a fixed penalty notice of £100. Failure to pay will make you liable to prosecution, where you could receive a fine of up to £1,000.

✓The law in much of this chapter could be set to change quite considerably in light of the Police, Crime, Sentencing and Courts Bill that Parliament is considering at the time of writing.

✓At the protest you may see individuals wearing hi-vis vests saying 'Legal Observer'. These individuals are trained volunteers who can assist you in knowing your legal rights. They will also monitor police behaviour and, if you are arrested, can help connect you with support in the police station. Be sure to be aware of the difference between Legal Observers and PCSOs: they often wear similar hi-vis jackets.

Protesting from home

Rent strikes

I write this in a year where students around the UK are arguing that they should not need to pay their accommodation costs as they haven't been at university due to the Covid-19 pandemic. Rent strikes seem more relevant than ever, and it's worth understanding the law.

Rent striking has no legal basis. The potential consequences are detailed below.

In short, if you are an assured tenant and the rent is unpaid for 8 weeks, the landlord can go to the court and the court must make an outright possession order. The landlord does not need to prove anything else. (See Chapter 1, on renting, for more on possession orders, evictions and assured tenancies. Chapter 1 relates to assured shorthold tenancies, which is a type of assured tenancy and by far the most common type of tenancy for private renters.)

Alongside their claim for possession, the landlord can also issue a claim for a County Court Judgment for the unpaid rent. In essence, the end result of this could mean you are kicked out of the property, and still need to pay the money you owe.

So why is a rent strike still seen as a popular form of activism? Well, if public opinion is on your side and you have a strong cause, the landlord might find themselves in an extremely difficult position if they were to actually take court action against you. A prime example might be if you are renting accommodation from a university and the university's poor treatment of the students is the basis of the rent strike. A university could potentially get awful press if it took legal action against its own students (especially when those students are already paying £9,000 per year) – as a result, and based upon the press attention that rent strikes frequently obtain, they can serve as an effective method of protest.

The Freedom of Information Act 2000

Freedom of information (FOI) requests are a key legal weapon in the protester's toolkit. They have revealed national scandals, from MPs' expenses to delays in handover between ambulance staff and A&E departments. It is a tool that seeks to ensure some level of transparency from government departments and other public authorities. Many are critical of its existence; however, it cannot be disputed that organisations are encouraged to act in more appropriate ways in the knowledge that an FOI request could require them to reveal certain information. If you want to uncover a big issue in society, having as much information as you can about it is often useful. An FOI request can sometimes help you get this added information.

Here is what you need to know if you wish to make an FOI request:

Which organisations can you request FOIs from?

If in doubt, you can query this with the Information Commissioner's Office (see p. 280). Broadly speaking, it is limited to public authorities. Examples of public authorities you can request information from are:

- the police service
- the fire service
- the NHS
- publicly owned companies
- local councils
- government departments

The full list can be found in Schedule 1 of the Freedom of Information Act 2000.

Making an FOI request

Before making a request, it is worth seeing if the request has been answered before. Life is too short to waste time. The organisation may have responses to previous FOI requests on their website. This will often be on a page of the website entitled 'disclosure log'. You can also search for many published responses to FOI requests on the gov.uk website. If an internet search doesn't bring up any results, you can always send an email to the organisation.

If you choose to make a request, you should give the following information:

- your name
- your contact details (for example your postal address or email address)
- a description of the information you want – the more detail you give, the better you can hope the response from the organisation will be

There are a number of ways you can make an FOI request. There is of course the conventional letter or email, but many organisations also have an online form where FOI requests can be made. You can also use social media. It may be a good idea to google 'how to access information from a public body' and click the ICO link before you make your request – just so you can be sure that you've ticked all the boxes when making your request.

✓ Feel free to request the response in a format that suits you. If you would prefer large print, or perhaps the response in an audio format – let them know!

What happens next?

You should receive the information within 20 working days of your request being received. That's not just an estimate: public authorities are required, under the wording of the Act, to respond within this time. If your request is to a school, you should note that they are allowed some extra time during the school holidays.

It can be disappointing when your request is refused. Sometimes, sensitive information is not available to the public. The organisation should let you know if this is the case when refusing your request.

Your request can also be refused if getting the information to you would cost a large amount of money.

✓ In terms of costs, while most requests will be free, the organisation may, on occasion, ask you to pay a small fee to account for things such as their photocopying and postage. The organisation will let you know if you need to pay anything.

11

On the Street

My grandmother recently learned how to text. Ever since, I receive regular variants of 'be safe'. You know – 'get home safely', 'safe travels', 'stay safe'. What does this actually mean, though? How precisely is one supposed to alter their behaviour in light of a 'be safe' text? I wonder if my gran knows herself?

Perhaps she doesn't, but her comments tap into an unconscious truth we are all aware of – whenever we leave the house, and are 'on the street', we never truly know what awaits us. You might bump into a man who has just won the lottery and gives you a hundred quid because you smiled at him. You might bump into a man who is drunk and decides to attack you. You literally don't know.

Grannies across the country are tapped into this.

We all lead different lives, and the 'stay safe' text from my gran might mean something different to the 'stay safe' text your gran sends you. For one granny 'stay safe' might mean hoping her grandson avoids street confrontations. For another, saying 'stay safe' might mean hoping her granddaughter, who has recently started wearing a hijab, remains vigilant of harassment she may encounter. To another, it might mean hoping her grandson remains calm and collected if he is stopped and searched by the police. We all have different realities, and this chapter reflects that.

Although granny might not think of it like this, I think she is encouraging you to be 'street wise'. In other words, she wants you to know how to avoid danger, but also to know what to do if it arises. A key way you can do this is by knowing your legal rights for when you are out and about. So, next time granny texts you saying, 'be safe lol xox', before you frustratedly remind her for the twentieth time that 'lol' does not stand for 'lots of love', instead simply interpret the text as 're-familiarise yourself with your legal rights before you step out of the door x'.

Self-defence

You're at the Red Dog pub waiting for friends and inadvertently catch the eye of a very drunk man. He approaches you and says, 'You're that idiot that crashed into the back of my car this morning!' This surprises you as you don't actually drive. Moments later you notice a clenched fist leaving the man's trouser pocket and instinctively know a punch towards your nose is pending. It looks like you might need to defend yourself. While most of us would hope never to be in this situation, it's true that we can rarely control others' behaviour. It is therefore helpful to know what you can do when confronted by someone else's violence.

The law on self-defence

- The law doesn't require you to wait to be struck first before you defend yourself. You can strike first if it is necessary.
- When defending yourself, you can use a *reasonable* amount of force, taking into account the circumstances you find yourself in.
- Force won't be considered reasonable if it wasn't needed. If the man is so drunk that he can't actually get his fist out of his pocket and is staggering so much that he will fall onto his bottom any second, delivering a flying-kick to his chest is unlikely to be considered reasonable. Therefore, if you can, take a moment to judge the severity of the situation.
- The law recognises that you may not be able to gauge the exact amount of force necessary in order to defend yourself in the face of an unexpected attack. It will take into account what you honestly and instinctively thought was necessary in the situation.
- You can also use reasonable force to defend somebody else.

Being stopped by the police

You're walking home alone at the end of a night out when a police van pulls up from behind, sirens blaring. Winding down the window, the officer on the passenger side says, 'Alright mate? I want to speak to you for a second.' The engine stops and the officer on the driver's side hops out and comes towards you.

You've done nothing wrong – why could the police possibly want to speak to you? You begin to feel panicked. What follows are three hypothetical scenarios you could be met with, and your rights in each.

1. Stop and account

A police officer or PCSO says, 'What's your name and where are you off to?'

This is called a 'stop and account'. You've simply been asked a question.

In the vast majority of situations, the police do not have the power to force you to stay in a stop and account. You also do not have to answer questions and, if there is no other reason to suspect you, you cannot be arrested for your refusal to do so.

A few exceptions you ought to know, though:

- If the police have reason to believe that you have been, or are, engaging in antisocial behaviour, you can be required to give your name and address, and it would be an offence to fail to do so.

- If the police have reasonable grounds for suspecting that you have committed an offence and it is necessary to arrest you to ascertain your name and address.

✓ If you are in doubt as to whether this is a stop and account or a stop and search, you can ask, 'Am I being detained?' If the answer is 'no', you can leave.

✓ If you do choose to answer the officer's questions, be aware that giving false information may amount to an offence – obstructing the police.

2. Stop and search

The officer says something broadly along the lines of 'Look mate – we've had reports of a tall white lad wearing a black puffer jacket stealing kids' phones on this street. You match the description. You are being detained for the purposes of a search.'

The minute you hear the word 'search', the acronym **WILD-R** should go through your head. For nearly any type of search, the police need to tell you the following:

- the reason why they want to search you (**Why?**)
- the officer's name and police station (**Identity?**)
- why they are legally allowed to search you (**Law?**)
- that you are being detained for the purposes of a search (**Detained?**)
- that you are entitled to have a copy of the search record (**Record?**)

Ideally, a police officer should just give you all this

information – it's their responsibility to tell you up front. If you notice that they've missed something, you can prompt them. You may even want to just go through WILD-R as a recap, to make sure you've understood and registered everything they've said – it's a helpful way to bring structure to a stressful experience. An exchange with the officer could go like this:

> You: *Why do you want to search me?*
> PO: *We suspect you may have stolen phones on you.*
> You: *What's your name and station number?*
> PO: *I'm PC [surname] from Police Station [name]*
> …
> You: *And can you tell me again the law that you are searching me under …*

The search in the scenario above is called a 'suspicion search'. In other words, the police have reason to suspect you as you match the description of the person they are looking for.

For this type of search, the police need reasonable grounds to suspect that you are carrying any of the following:

- drugs
- a weapon
- stolen property
- something that can be used to commit a crime, such as a crowbar

3. Without suspicion search

Before giving the officer a chance to get a word out you say, 'I haven't done anything wrong!' He responds, 'We are not saying you have – but we are going to need to search you anyway.'

As with an ordinary stop and search, the moment you hear the word 'search', the WILD-R acronym should go through your head.

The police can only search an individual without suspicion in very limited circumstances – most commonly when a Section 60 authorisation (or 'Section 60 order') is in place.

If, when you get to the 'law' part of WILD-R, they don't mention Section 60 (and haven't said why they are searching you), you may want to make sure that you do indeed obtain a record of your search as you may have grounds for a complaint later.

A Section 60 authorisation enables the police to search anybody in a defined area for a specific time period: no longer than 24 hours (but this can be extended). This could be anyone from your 13-year-old nephew to your middle-aged mother. The usual requirements of reasonable suspicion do not apply.

A Section 60 authorisation can only be put in place if a senior officer reasonably believes that:

- an incident involving serious violence may take place in an area, and authorisation of Section 60 will help to prevent this; or

- an incident involving serious violence **has** taken place in an area and the weapon used in the incident is being carried in the area, and authorisation of Section 60 will help find the weapon; or
- people are carrying weapons in the area without good reason.

Police must make efforts to advise the public when a Section 60 order is in place – for example through social media. Nonetheless, despite best efforts, there is every possibility a Section 60 may be in place in your area at a given time and you do not know.

Here is an example of a tweet from Lambeth Police in relation to Section 60, accompanied by an image of a map of part of South London.

@LambethMPS (Aug 10, 2019)

A Section 60 has been implemented in the areas below from 1900 until 0600 Sunday morning. This follows violence in the area earlier this evening. This gives police increased stop & search powers to help keep the peace.

What exactly can the officer search?

For all the above types of searches, what exactly the officer can search depends on whether you are in public or private.

In public

Let's say you are in public. In this case, the officer can only require you to remove outer clothing. A good way to think of outer clothing is the type of clothing you would immediately take off if it had been a cold day outside and you entered a warm room. So, gloves, jacket, coat.

They can also ask you to turn out your pockets, check your bags, and feel around the inside of your collar, socks and shoes. Feeling in the inside of a collar or sock could mean they are physically touching your skin.

Outside of public view

If an officer wants you to remove more than just your outer clothing, this must be done outside of public view. Also, the officer doing the search must be of the same sex as you. Further still, no person of the opposite sex should be in the presence of the search – unless you request it.

Outside of public view could mean being searched at a police station or in a police van. It *does not* include an empty street.

If you cover your head or face for religious reasons – for example you are a Sikh man, Rastafarian man or Muslim woman – and the police have reason to ask you to remove this headwear, they should allow you to remove it outside of public view. Where practicable, the police officer doing the search should be the same sex as you, and the search should take place outside of the sight of anybody of the opposite sex.

✓If a Section 60 authorisation is in force, or a Section 60AA authorisation has been given (which gives the police the specific power to require the removal of 'disguises'), the police have the power to require the removal of any item that they reasonably believe you are wearing to conceal your identity – even if in public.

What is included in a record of search?

The search record must contain:

- the officer's details
- the date, time and location of the stop and search
- the reason for the stop and search and its outcome
- your name, or your description if you have refused to give your name
- your ethnicity
- what the officer found and what they were looking for
- your vehicle registration number (if relevant)

It's nearly always worth asking for a copy of the search record (a receipt) following a stop and search. This will assist if you want to make a complaint at a later date. It is important to ask for this even if you don't feel angry at the time. Feelings can change and it is important you have as much evidence as possible if you do choose to complain. Although you may be asked to, you do not have to give your name to the police in order for them to provide you with a receipt.

Being stopped and searched if transgender

You may find a stop and search particularly invasive if you are transgender. It is important to know that when it comes to searches able to be done in public, you can ask to be searched by an officer of the same gender you identify with, and if it is reasonably practicable, this should be done. If the police wish to do a search that would need to be done outside of public view, you can insist that they recognise your gender so that you are searched by an officer of the appropriate gender. You can also ask the officer to address you with the pronouns you feel comfortable with.

✓ At the time of writing, organisation Y-Stop have an app that lets you record a stop and search, making it easier for you to complain if you feel you have been wrongly stopped and searched. See y-stop.org.

What are my rights if the police stop me while I am driving?

The police can stop your car for any reason. They don't need to suspect you've done something wrong. If you don't stop when requested to do so, you are breaking the law.

The police can ask to see your driving licence, insurance certificate and MOT certificate. If these documents are not with you, you have 7 days to take them to a police station. If you do not do so, you break the law.

In terms of searching you or your car, the police cannot do this unless the grounds for stop and search apply – for example, they have reasonable grounds to suspect that weapons or drugs are in the vehicle.

Can the police enter my home?

The general rule is that the police are not able to enter your home unless they have your permission or a warrant for your arrest from the court. However, in some circumstances the police have a power of entry even if you do not give permission or they do not have a warrant.

The most common reasons are as follows:

- To deal with or prevent a breach of the peace.
- To save life or limb.
- To prevent serious damage to the property.
- To recapture somebody who has escaped from custody.
- To arrest a person in connection with an indictable offence (indictable offences are the most serious types of offences, which must be heard in the Crown Court; but in the context being used here, also include less serious offences that *can* be heard in the Crown Court, but don't have to be. An example is the offence of theft, which can be heard in either the magistrates' court or the Crown Court depending on factors such as the seriousness of the specific circumstances).

In terms of when the police can search your property – they can do so to the extent that is required for the purpose for which the power of entry was exercised. In plain English, let's say the police enter the property 'to save life or limb' as they believe somebody is about to be shot – they would probably be able to search the house for the gun that they believe would be used.

In addition, the police can search any premises occupied or controlled by a person who is under arrest for an indictable offence, provided the officer has reasonable grounds for suspecting that there is evidence on the premises relating either to the offence the person has been arrested for, or another indictable offence which is connected with or similar to that offence. The search can only be to the extent that is reasonably required to discover such evidence.

Arresting a fellow citizen

You're walking the dog and see a man steal an elderly woman's handbag. The woman shouts 'stop that man!'

Are you able to intervene? Here's the law.

When we think of arrest, we usually think of an act done by the police – but you, as a citizen, can in some circumstances arrest another citizen.

Now, if you see someone drop their crisp packet on the floor – this isn't cause for you to arrest them.

Importantly, the law states that the offence in question has to be an indictable offence in order for you to arrest another citizen (see above, 'Can the police enter my home?', for the meaning of 'indictable offence' in this context).

The power to arrest another citizen is substantial. That's why the law makes it clear that, in order to carry one out, it needs to appear to you that it is not reasonably practicable for a police officer to make the arrest instead. This makes sense. Citizens diving in to arrest people when a police officer is literally stood next to them is not the intention here.

In order to arrest, you need to have reasonable grounds for believing that the arrest is necessary to prevent the person you are planning to arrest from:

- causing physical injury to himself or any other person;
- suffering physical injury;
- causing loss of or damage to property; or
- making off before a police officer can assume responsibility for him.

In terms of the level of force you can use, it is 'reasonable force'. **If you use more force than is deemed reasonable, there is a very real risk that *you* end up being the one charged with assault!**

✓ It is important that you inform the person of the fact that you are arresting them as soon as is practicable (whether this being at the time of arrest or as soon as you can afterwards). You also need to tell them why you are arresting them. There isn't a need for any precise wording – just make it clear. Want to know more on all of this? Have a read of Section 24A of the Police and Criminal Evidence Act 1984.

12

The Justice System

This chapter comes at the end of the book for a reason. In almost every other chapter I've mentioned the possibility of going to court, and your right to pursue justice, as well as the potential that you may yourself face prosecution or have somebody make a claim against you. Whether you've chosen to write to your landlord, lodge a complaint about discrimination, or been arrested at a protest, here is where you will find the information relevant to when – whether through your own choice or circumstance – you come into contact with the law, or it looks as if you soon might.

This is the chapter that I hope can serve you when you feel particularly downtrodden, tired and frankly fed up. It is a chapter designed to hold your hand when going through some of life's tougher moments. In these moments, it's not good enough to just 'hope it will all be alright'. This chapter will give you tips to help you if you ever find yourself in a courtroom. It should also be the chapter running through your mind if you ever find yourself in a police station, not knowing what your legal rights are. If you are a freelancer and tired of not being paid for your work, it is this chapter that can steer you in the right direction in terms of steps to take.

Knowledge really is power and it is hoped that this chapter will give you the tools to face, confront and take control of the situation you find yourself in.

Steps to take when considering legal action

Taking legal action is a big step. Not only can it be time consuming, but expensive too. Most issues won't ever need to be considered by a court if you take the time to do some of the things within this section.

Writing a good letter of complaint

Every now and then, we need to write a good old formal letter of complaint. It might be to our landlord, a retailer, or to a public authority such as a hospital. Letters are effective because they show you're serious, they put your issues in writing and they can be used as evidence at a later date.

Here are tried and tested things to include in your letter of complaint to give it maximum punch.

Explain what happened and the impact it is having on you

You want to be as clear as possible. You want to limit any delays from the other side asking for clarification about a matter. For example, if you purchased some sort of product that is faulty, quote the serial number and just about anything else that identifies that exact product. Describe exactly in what way it is faulty and what this means for you (for example, the 'on' switch on your kettle is stuck, meaning you cannot flick it downwards to turn the kettle on and can no longer boil water). Be sure to mention any distress or inconvenience you have suffered too.

Explain exactly what you want to happen now

Having explained what has happened and the impact it is having, you can now address what you want to happen. If you are asking for a certain amount of money back, explain how you have come to this figure. Attach proof (e.g. receipts) if you can. It is important to be clear – if, for example, you are living in rented accommodation and your boiler has broken, be clear as to whether you are asking for your landlord to fix it, or to reimburse you for the cost of getting someone in to fix it.

Include evidence and refer to previous correspondence

If there were any discussions you had with the individual (or representative from the company) that were not in writing, you may want to incorporate them into the letter now so that you start building up a paper trail. For example, if writing a letter to your landlord, you could say, 'On 3 February while at the property, you confirmed that you would fix the broken latch on the bedroom window by the 18 February.' This is important because – let's say matters go to court and the court sees the letters that have been sent between the two of you – if the landlord has not responded making an issue of your assertion in relation to the bedroom window latch, it supports the view that this conversation *did* take place, and isn't one conveniently being made up now in an attempt to exaggerate your landlord's incompetence.

- If applicable, explain the law that supports your argument. This book can hopefully give you a steer, but do wider reading.
- State a deadline by which you expect them to reply – in many instances, 14 days will be deemed 'reasonable'.
- If the circumstances warrant it, explain that you will start court proceedings if you do not receive a response.
- Include your contact information so they can get back to you.

✓ The circumstances may dictate whether it is more appropriate to send your letter through the post or as an email. If using post, it a good idea to send it using recorded delivery – that way, you will be notified when it is delivered. This makes it clear that you are serious but also puts pressure on the organisation/individual to actually respond. They can't just say it got lost in the post.

✓ Stick to the facts. Avoid being sarcastic or angry. Especially if you are writing to a large company – the person who reads your letter probably isn't the person at fault and getting their back up is not going to help you. You want the person reading your letter to understand where you are coming from so that progress can be made.

Writing a subject access request (SAR)

You have the right to obtain a copy of the personal data an organisation holds about you, in addition to other supplementary information.

The Information Commissioner's Office (ICO) website contains a free handy and easily understandable guide on how to make a subject access request (see p. 280).

Despite this handy guide, it is important to know that no particular format is necessary to make a subject access request. A request will be valid so long as you make it clear that you are asking for your own personal data and the organisation is able to confirm your identity. It can be made both verbally and in writing – even over social media. A written request is probably the best idea as this ensures a proper record of your request. It would also be sensible to use a heading such as 'subject access request' in your letter or in the email subject field, just so the organisation cannot say they were in any way confused with the nature of the request.

An organisation will usually need to respond to your request within 1 month. If they need more time, they should inform you of this within this 1-month period, letting you know the reasons why.

If you do not receive a response from the organisation or are dissatisfied with it, you should first complain to the organisation. If you remain unhappy, you can complain to the ICO (see p. 280).

How to have a firm but fair conversation with somebody holding a balance of power

Whether it be your landlord or your boss (or perhaps a colleague at your workplace), a good conversation can resolve a lot.

Important things to remember:

- be prepared – it can be a good idea to write a note to yourself of what exactly you plan to say during the conversation. This can help you communicate your message more clearly and also help you remember everything
- don't be aggressive
- stick to the facts
- show evidence
- be aware of your rights in the situation and, politely, remind the other person about these if needs be

What makes good evidence

If you do take your case to court, you will be asked to provide evidence. You will also likely be asked for evidence if you make a complaint to an organisation or an individual. You never quite know when such situations might occur, so it is always a good idea to keep records of things. Depending on the situation, here are things that count as good evidence:

- receipts
- photos
- tickets
- email exchanges
- screenshots of messages
- recordings (where appropriate)
- a written diary/log of incidents. For example, if the incident is to do with a neighbour being noisy, a note of the dates and times when the noises occurred. Although this evidence may be weak on its own (it's just your writing), it can help build a bigger picture. You may also find that it helps bolster evidence you come into further downstream.

Three key principles to adopt so that you always have a steady stream of evidence ready if needed:

1. Discuss things in writing rather than verbally. This means there is a record.
2. Whenever a conversation of importance takes place verbally, follow it up with something in writing which details the content of the conversation. Let's say it relates to your landlord, Nicole. You could simply send a polite message afterwards saying, 'Hi Nicole, good speaking to you today and thank you for agreeing to fix the toilet by 3 March. Many thanks.' Your landlord will likely respond 'Thanks' – and you now have a message trail that you could use as evidence that the landlord confirmed she would fix your toilet by 3 March.

3. Whenever you obtain a receipt or ticket, make it a habit to snap a photo of it.

Alternative dispute resolution

Alternative dispute resolution schemes may enable you to resolve a dispute without needing to go to court. They can save considerable time and money when compared with court action. Some examples of alternatives to court that you may wish to consider are as follows:

Mediation is when a neutral third party (a mediator) assists you and the party you are in dispute with in finding a solution that you both agree to. Both parties need to agree to mediate before the mediation can take place. The mediator will not take sides, nor can they impose their own solution. It is an interactive and structured process. Mediation need not be legally binding, but can be if both parties agree to this. Find out more at civilmediation.org.

Arbitration is a more formal type of alternative dispute resolution. You and the party you are in dispute with will put your case to an independent person, known as an arbitrator. Both you and the party you are in dispute with will need to agree to this process before it can take place. The arbitrator will then make a decision which is legally binding. Find out more at ciarb.org.

Ombudsman schemes investigate and resolve complaints. There are different ombudsman schemes covering various different sectors – for example, there is the Financial Ombudsman Service that can help sort out unresolved complaints you have with a bank, and the Rail Ombudsman that can assist with unresolved complaints with a train provider. You must have first tried to sort things out using the internal complaints procedure of the service provider in question before you refer a matter to the ombudsman. Whether a decision will be binding will depend on a number of factors. You can speak with the ombudsman service in question about this. Find out more at ombudsmanassociation.org.

Making a small claim

Making a small claim is a relatively easy way to take action against an individual or firm. A small claim could be appropriate in a number of different scenarios. Commonly, they will be used where somebody owes you money for some work you did, you've received a poor service somewhere, you've purchased something turning out to be faulty, or you're in a dispute with your landlord.

The typical limit for a small claim is £10,000 (but if you're asking your landlord to carry out repairs, the work needs to cost less than £1,000).

The process is intended to be as simple as possible, and many people will go through it without a solicitor.

If you want to make a small claim, search online for 'making a small claim' and follow the link to the gov.uk website where you can get more information. The charity

Advicenow (contact information on p. 277) provide guidance on their website about running small claims cases. The Civil Procedure Rules which apply to small claims are publicly available on the Ministry of Justice website. Simply google 'civil procedure rules' and click the justice.gov.uk link.

Although not particularly complicated, making a small claim can be time consuming and costs money – in fact, if the amount it will cost you isn't much less than the amount you hope to get back, you may want to consider whether it is worth it in the first place. If you win your case you will often be able to get the fees you paid back, but if you lose, you may have to pay some of the other side's expenses! Furthermore, if the person doesn't actually have the money to pay, there's every chance you won't get it back even if you go through court (or, if they have some money but not all of it, it might take a number of years to receive the money as the court may allow them to pay in small instalments). As a result it is nearly always a good idea to try to solve things without involving the court if possible. Consider some of the steps to take before going to court suggested earlier in this chapter.

Usually you will have 6 years to take legal action. Remember: courts deal with evidence. Therefore, making your claim closer to the date the issue took place may mean you have more of the all-important evidence, such as tickets and receipts.

If you are in the criminal justice system

Your rights in police custody

You have the right to:

- **An interpreter.** If English is not your first language, ensure you request an interpreter. Do not be deterred because you are told it may delay the process. It is important you understand everything you are being told. If you are deaf, you are entitled to a signer.
- **Free legal advice.** Simply ask for the 'duty solicitor'. They are independent of the police and available 24 hours a day. Do not be deterred because you are told it may delay the process – it is always wise to be interviewed having obtained advice from a legal professional first. If you do not get legal advice and end up being charged, you may regret not having sought advice in the first place.
- **Obtain medical help if you are feeling unwell.** You will not be charged for the healthcare professional coming to see you. You should also inform the police immediately if you require any medication.
- **Ask that the police call someone for you to let them know where you are.** This could, for example, be a friend or a family member. It is completely free. Ask the police to contact your consulate or embassy if you are not from the UK.
- **See a written notice informing you of your rights.** If

you do not speak English, you can ask for this notice in your language. It is helpful to familiarise yourself with this document.

- **Look at the 'Codes of Practice'.** These are rules that the police are to follow. They are quite dense so it is a good idea to be familiar with them *before* you need to be. To find the Codes, google 'police and criminal evidence act 1984 codes of practice', and click on the gov.uk link. Quite a few different Codes will come up which are all worth a read. Code C is the one to read if you want information on the rules the police are to follow while you are in police custody.

If your child (under 18) is in police custody

- The police must attempt to contact you.
- Your child must be interviewed with an appropriate adult present. This will usually be **you** as the parent, guardian or carer.

How long can I be kept in custody?

Generally, you cannot be held for more than 24 hours without being charged with a crime. If you are suspected of a serious crime, for example murder, detention may be authorised for up to 36 hours. Before the 36 hours expires, the police can make an application to the magistrates' court for a warrant of further detention. This can extend the detention by another 36 hours, which makes 72 hours in total. The police can make an application to the magistrates' court to extend the warrant once again. The maximum period of detention without charge is 96 hours.

If you are arrested under the Terrorism Act, you can be held for up to 14 days without charge.

Your rights when being questioned

You have the right to have your solicitor present with you in the interview and of course an interpreter if English is not your first language.

You have the right to request that the interview be paused so that you can obtain further legal advice from your solicitor at any point during the interview.

You have the right to remain silent. Before the interview starts, you will be cautioned. This means the police will say to you the following:

> You do not have to say anything. But it may harm your defence if you do not mention when questioned something which you later rely on in court. Anything you do say may be given in evidence.

While the wording of the caution makes it abundantly clear that you have a right to remain silent, it is important to be aware of the consequences of doing so.

For example, if at the police station, the following exchange takes place:

> Police: *Why were you in the dark alley where the drugs were located?*

You: *No comment.*

And at court, the following exchange takes place:

Your barrister: *Why were you in the dark alley where the drugs were located?*
You: *I thought I had dropped my phone in the alley the night before, so I went back there to check.*

Because you did not give this explanation in interview, the court is permitted to draw what is called an 'adverse inference' against you. This means it could potentially hold your silence in interview against you. It may think, 'you were silent in your police interview because you didn't have a good explanation, and now you are making up a story'.

Voluntary interviews

There may be instances where the police contact you and ask you to attend the police station for a voluntary interview to assist them with an investigation. This could be done, for example, where the police do not have sufficient evidence to arrest you, or don't think it is necessary to do so. Voluntary interviews should be treated seriously. You will be interviewed under caution, meaning anything you say could be used in court against you if you are later arrested and charged with an offence. You have the right to leave a voluntary interview at any time and also to know why the police want to interview you. You also do not have to attend a voluntary interview. You are entitled to free legal advice before your voluntary interview and for a solicitor to be present with you during the voluntary interview.

At court

Advice for victims of crime and prosecution witnesses

- A 'witness care officer' should keep you informed of which court you will need to go to and when. Let them know well in advance if you anticipate there being any issues with your attendance – it may be that transport can be arranged for you or you can give your evidence over a video link. Other special measures may be available to you too, such as a screen or curtain being placed around the witness box so that, when you are giving your evidence, the defendant cannot see you. This might be of particular benefit if you are fearful of the defendant.
- Due to the time that may have elapsed between the incident and the trial, your recall of events may have faded a little. You are able to ask the Crown Prosecution Service to show you your statement so that you can refresh your memory before going into court.
- You will usually have a room separate from where the public are so that you needn't have to worry about bumping into the defendant or any of his/her associates.
- If you are a victim you can make something called a 'victim impact statement'. This is where you can set out how the offence that took place has affected you. You can

be very raw and honest in this. If following being mugged you are fearful of going outside after dark, you can say this. You can either read your statement out in court yourself, or ask somebody else to do it for you. It is the court's decision as to whether your statement will be read out in its entirety, or just part of it.

Advice for defence witnesses

- The defendant's lawyer will inform you of when you will be required to attend court. If you anticipate any issues, speak to the lawyer as far in advance as you can so that there is time for them to be addressed. You may be able to claim expenses for your court-related travel – speak to the defendant's lawyer about this.

Advice for defendants

- Familiarise yourself with the layout of the courtroom and how to address the different people in the court. Getting these basics right can help calm your nerves.
- Try to keep calm, even if things are being said about you that you know are not true. Allowing your emotions to dominate your focus can make it difficult to absorb what is being said. You will be much better placed to give your best evidence if you have been able to remain calm throughout.

Criminal records

You may be unsure if you actually have a criminal record. A way you can check is by making a subject access request. This is where you can request a copy of the information an organisation holds on you (see p. 263). You should make your request to the ACRO Criminal Records Office.

When you are applying for a job, prospective employers are able to check your criminal record. This is known as a Disclosure and Barring Service (DBS) check.

There are different 'types' of checks that can be done.

Type of check	*What it shows*
Basic	Unspent convictions and conditional cautions
Standard	Spent and unspent convictions, cautions, reprimands, final warnings
Enhanced	Same as standard check + information that may be considered relevant to the role held by local police forces
Enhanced with barred lists	Same as enhanced check + whether you are on the list of people barred from doing the role – typically these lists will include those who have been barred from working with vulnerable adults or barred from working with children

✓ Under an enhanced DBS check, provided it is deemed relevant to the role you are applying for, the police are able to disclose *any* information on their database about you – even if you were never convicted or cautioned in relation to the matter. It is a matter for your prospective employer how much weight they choose to place upon the information. Some of the organisations listed at the back of the book will be able to provide further information on DBS checks if this is of concern.

On many job application forms and role specifications you will see the type of DBS check required. There is a gov. uk webpage dedicated to detailing when convictions become spent, so you can see how it applies in your own case.

If you are transgender and do not want your prospective employer to be aware of your previous identity, you can contact the 'DBS sensitive applications team' for assistance. An internet search will uncover the details of this service.

If you think your DBS certificate displays incorrect information, there is a gov.uk webpage where you can fill out a form and report the issue. This applies to standard and enhanced DBS checks. Google 'report a problem about a criminal record check or barring decision'.

✓ The organisation Business in the Community have on their website a list of employers who have signed up to their 'Ban the Box' campaign. These employers, unlike many others, will not require individuals to tick a box stating whether or not they have a criminal conviction at the application stage. Candidates will instead be asked about such matters later on in the recruitment process. Google 'business in the community ban the box' for more information.

Useful Organisations

This list is not exhaustive and there are, no doubt, brilliant organisations that have not been included. It simply seeks to point you in the right direction if you would value some additional support having read this book.

Acas

Provide impartial and free advice for employers and employees on their rights. Their website contains a number of helpful guides on different employment law matters and they have a helpline where you can discuss matters with them.

0300 123 1100

www.acas.org.uk

Advicenow

Website providing practical information on rights and the law in England and Wales. It is run by the charity Law for Life. The Advicenow website contains helpful guides on going to a civil court and also information on how to deal with benefit problems.

www.advicenow.org.uk

Alcohol Change UK

Charity aiming to reduce the harm caused by alcohol. Their website contains useful material if you or a loved one require support with an alcohol problem.

0203 907 8480 (this is for general enquiries and is not a helpline number. Drinkline is the national alcohol helpline, who can be contacted on 0300 123 1100)

www.alcoholchange.org.uk

Citizens Advice

Your local bureau can offer you confidential advice or signpost you to organisations that may be able to help. The Citizens Advice website also contains helpful information in relation to a wide variety of legal topics.

0800 144 8848 (England)

0800 702 2020 (Wales)

www.citizensadvice.org.uk

Crisis

Charity offering support, advice and courses for the homeless. They have 'skylight centres' across the country where they offer different types of education, training and support to those who are homeless or at risk of homelessness.

0300 636 1967

www.crisis.org.uk

The Crown Prosecution Service

The website of the Crown Prosecution Service details how criminal cases will be prosecuted. It is a useful website to peruse if you are appearing in court and want to get a sense of the types of arguments that lawyers will be making.

www.cps.gov.uk

The Defendant

Organisation providing emotional and practical support to defendants in criminal law proceedings. Their website contains helpful information for anybody seeking to better understand the different stages of the criminal justice system.

07938 859988
info@thedefendant.org.uk
www.thedefendant.org.uk

DrugWise

Organisation providing advice and information in relation to drugs, alcohol and tobacco. Their website provides helpful information in relation to a range of different types of drugs.

www.drugwise.org.uk

FRANK

Anti-drug advisory service whose website contains information in relation to drugs – from maximum sentences, to their effects on the body. Their website has an online chat function and a contact section where you can ask a question and receive a response via email.

0300 123 6600

Text 82111
www.talktofrank.com

GOV.UK

Official government website containing useful information on a broad range of topics.
www.gov.uk

Green & Black Cross

Independent grassroots project. Their website contains an array of useful resources worth reviewing before attending a protest.
www.greenandblackcross.org

The Information Commissioner's Office (ICO)

The ICO is the UK's independent body set up to uphold information rights. Their website contains user-friendly guides on a number of matters relating to data privacy. You will also find information on how to make a complaint to an organisation in relation to your personal data.
0303 123 1113
www.ico.org.uk

INQUEST

Charity specialising in state-related deaths, in particular deaths occurring in state custody and detention. Their website contains helpful factsheets and a handbook to assist those going through the inquest process.
0207 263 1111
www.inquest.org.uk

The Law Society

The independent professional body for solicitors. Their website contains a useful 'find a solicitor' search function for members of the public. This can enable you to find a suitably qualified solicitor for your issue.

www.solicitors.lawsociety.org.uk

Liberty

Civil liberties organisation that provide helpful explainers on numerous legal topics. They also offer an 'advice and information' service where they respond to queries from the public on their legal rights.

www.libertyhumanrights.org.uk

Mind

Charity providing advice and support to those experiencing a mental health problem. Their website contains helpful information on a number of issues related to mental health.

0300 123 3393
info@mind.org.uk
www.mind.org.uk

MoneySavingExpert.com

Website providing useful information on all things spending and money. There are a number of useful guides on their website which can help you stand up to authority.

www.moneysavingexpert.com

National Debtline

Charity providing debt advice. Their website contains a number of informative fact sheets on different matters relating to debt, along with a tool that can help you work out your budget. There is also an online chat function.
0808 808 4000
www.nationaldebtline.org

NHS online information

Website containing reliable information on a number of health matters – from an explanation of different medical conditions, to details about different medications and their side effects.
www.nhs.uk

Ofgem

The government regulator for gas and electricity markets in Great Britain. Their website contains useful information for gas and electricity consumers – from videos aimed at helping you understand your bills, to a page dedicated to key terms that you can review if there are words that you don't understand in relation to your gas or electricity. Their website also provides guidance on steps to take to complain about a bill or your supplier.
www.ofgem.gov.uk

POhWER

Charity providing information, advice, support and advocacy to individuals who experience disability, distress, vulnerability and

social exclusion. Among other services, they provide Independent Mental Health Advocacy. They also have a podcast.
0300 456 2370
www.pohwer.net

Refuge

Charity providing advice and information to women and children facing domestic abuse.
National Domestic Abuse Helpline: 0808 200 0247
www.refuge.org.uk

Release

Charity providing free and impartial advice and information on issues relating to drug use and drug laws.
0207 324 2989
ask@release.org.uk
www.release.org.uk

Respect / Respect Men's Advice Line

Charity providing services for victims of domestic abuse, including a helpline for victims whether male or female, and one specifically for male victims.
0808 802 4040 (helpline for victims of domestic abuse and those supporting them)
0808 801 0327 (helpline for men who are facing domestic abuse)
info@respect.uk.net / info@mensadviceline.org.uk
www.respect.uk.net
www.mensadviceline.org.uk

Rethink Mental Illness

Charity providing advice and support to those experiencing a mental health problem. Their website contains helpful information on a number of issues related to mental health.

0808 801 0525

www.rethink.org

Samaritans

Charity providing emotional support to anyone in emotional distress, struggling to cope, or at risk of suicide. Their phoneline is open at all hours.

116 123

www.samaritans.org

The Sentencing Council

The website of the Sentencing Council contains 'Sentencing Guidelines' for each offence. If you type the name of an offence along with the words 'sentencing guidelines' into a search engine, the relevant page of the Sentencing Council will usually appear. Here, you can see what the courts will have in mind when passing a sentence.

www.sentencingcouncil.org.uk

Shelter Cymru

Charity providing services for people in Wales going through housing issues. Their website is a useful resource for information relating to housing. They have centres across the country and a helpline if in need of urgent housing advice.

0800 049 5495
www.sheltercymru.org.uk

Shelter England

Charity providing services for people in England going through housing issues. Their website is a useful resource for information relating to housing. They have centres across the country, a helpline if in need of urgent housing advice and an online chat function.
0808 800 4444
www.england.shelter.org.uk

StepChange

Service providing debt advice. Their website contains a significant amount of information about different aspects of debt. There is also an online chat function and a budget template that you can download and print.
0800 138 1111
www.stepchange.org

StopWatch

Organisation campaigning against the disproportionate use of stop and search. Their website contains useful information on police powers.
0208 226 5737
www.stop-watch.org

Unlock

Charity providing advice for people with criminal records. Their website contains helpful information on DBS checks and when convictions will become 'spent'.

www.unlock.org.uk

Victim Support

Charity offering support to victims of crime. They have a 24/7 helpline and an online live chat service.

0808 168 9111

www.victimsupport.org.uk

Which?

Website containing helpful information on a comprehensive range of consumer rights related issues.

www.which.co.uk

Women's Aid

Charity offering advice and information to women and children facing domestic abuse. They have a confidential online chat function on their website where you can discuss issues you may be facing.

info@womensaid.org.uk

www.womensaid.org.uk

Acknowledgements

It was important to me that this book was both legal and practical. As I said in the introduction, my expertise does not span every topic. Therefore I would like to thank the experts who reviewed the information I collated for each chapter. Not only have they been generous with their time, but their professional anecdotes have enabled the inclusion of practical tips that I hope can be of value to readers.

For their expert contribution, I want to thank the following individuals and organisations: Michael Abiodun Olatokun, Head of Public and Youth Engagement at the Bingham Centre for the Rule of Law, and Professor Tom Lewis, Director of the Centre for Rights and Justice, Nottingham Law School (Preface: Your Human Rights); John Gallagher, Principal Solicitor at Shelter, Gary Willock, barrister, and Daniella Weduwer at Energy UK (Chapter 1: Renting); Mark George QC, barrister, and JUNO Women's Aid (Chapter 2: Relationships); Hannah Laithwaite, barrister (Chapter 3: Shopping);

Feroz Bhimani, solicitor at Caines Law, the British Parking Association, and Judith Turner, Deputy Chief Ombudsman at the Rail Ombudsman (Chapter 4: Transport); Dr Jonathan L. Murray, sessional GP working in Nottingham, Dr Alicia Skervin, General Surgical Registrar at East Surrey Hospital, and Ann Bessell, social worker (Chapter 5: Healthcare); The National Association of Student Money Advisers (NASMA), Jonathan Chesterman, Debt Advice Policy Manager at Step-Change, and Gregory Butera (Chapter 6: Money); Bayo Randle, barrister, and Dr Peter McTigue, Senior Lecturer at Nottingham Law School (Chapter 7: Employment); Niamh Eastwood, Executive Director of Release, Richard Piper, CEO of Alcohol Change UK, Clare Ashcroft, barrister, and Harry Shapiro, Director of DrugWise (Chapter 8: Alcohol and Other Drugs); Melissa Stock, barrister and founder of the Privacy Law Barrister blog, Olivia Wint, Data Protection Manager, Nailah Ukaidi, Data Protection & Privacy Consultant, and Benson Egwuonwu, solicitor (Chapter 9: The Digital World); Mira Hammad, barrister, Green & Black Cross, and Activist Court Aid Brigade (Chapter 10: Activism); Mark George QC, barrister, and the Network for Police Monitoring (Netpol) (Chapter 11: On the Street); Mark George QC, barrister, Greater Manchester Law Centre, and Simon Pook, Civil Liberties Solicitor at Robert Lizar Solicitors (Chapter 12: The Justice System).

I would also like to thank all the staff at Garden Court North Chambers, along with my family, friends and other lawyers who have provided encouragement and support throughout this process. Not only have they assisted with ad hoc responses to queries, but many have connected me to experts able to review chapters where my own networks have not stretched so far.

Starting on p. 277, I offer a list of resources that, like this book, I hope you find useful. If you disagree with something I have said or think it could have been explained more clearly, do let me know – I am always learning. I would also add, of course, that the views expressed in this book are my own, and any errors – of fact or judgement – are entirely my responsibility.

Thanks are also due to those who have helped me along my journey of professional development and with The Law in 60 Seconds more generally – in particular Julie Higginbottom and Melanie King of Nottingham Law School, Clare Ashcroft of Garden Court North Chambers and His Honour John Samuels QC.

The Law in 60 Seconds: A Pocket Guide to Your Rights would not exist without the support of my editor, Louisa Dunnigan of Profile Books, and my literary agent, Nicola Chang. Louisa's meticulous reading cannot be overstated, and her suggestions have enabled me to articulate points far better than had I been left to my own devices. Nicola played an invaluable role in moulding the initial idea for this book and has supported and continues to support my vision of making the law more accessible. I would also like to thank my copyeditor, Patrick Taylor, whose careful reading in the final stages has helped me, hopefully, to create a book that is as readable as possible.

Finally, I must thank my parents, who, throughout the writing of this book, have observed an increasingly recluse version of their son, but as ever, have remained tirelessly supportive and encouraging.